M000231807

Discernment Do's and Don'ts

Discernment Do's and Don'ts

A Practical Guide to Vocational Discernment

Fr. George Elliott

TAN Books
Charlotte, North Carolina

Praise for Discernment Do's and Don'ts

"Father George Elliott's *Discernment Do's and Don'ts* is an excellent and accessible guide to vocational discernment. Though many pitfalls await young people discerning their vocation in the modern world, God unfailingly calls each of us to love Him in a particular state of life. Father Elliott's work draws on sound doctrine, the writings of the saints, and his own experience to help those who are discerning their vocation to avoid common pitfalls and to respond to God's call with an undivided heart. God gives His grace in abundance to those who respond generously to His call, just as Saint Paul tells us, "in everything God works for good with those who love Him, who are called according to His purpose" (Rom 8:28). Father Elliott's book is an important help in seeking and responding to God's grace given to us, so that we may know our vocation in life and respond to it with all our heart.

"In continuity with *Pastores Dabo Vobis*, the new *Ratio Fundamentalis Institutionis Sacerdotalis* states that, it is the mission of the Church "to care for the birth, discernment and fostering of vocations, particularly those to the priesthood" (RF, 13). Furthermore, it identifies the future priest as a 'man of discernment' (RF, 43). With this present book, inspired from these Ecclesial Documents and from his own personal experience, Fr. George presents us with a timely and practical guide to vocational discernment. This insightful work will undoubtedly assist men and women to discern the will of God in their lives, while humbly, confidently, and joyfully submitting themselves to His divine plan in creating and redeeming them, so that they may share with Him in glory for all eternity."

—Archbishop Jorge Patrón-Wong, Secretary for
Seminaries, Congregation for the Clergy

"As I personally discerned priesthood and, for over a decade, accompanied many university students through their personal journey of vocational discernment, I wish I would have had as much practical advice at my fingertips as this book provides. Fr. Elliott has done a fantastic job of compiling the most important principles to keep in mind while one is trying to figure out God's will for their vocation. The personal insights are fantastic and certainly resonate with my journey which eventually led me to the vocation of marriage."

—Jeff Runyan, Sr. Director of International Relations – Fellowship of Catholic University Students (FOCUS)

"In a world in which the very idea of 'vocation' is a counter-cultural concept, many parents and educators need support in encouraging young people to open their hearts and hear God's voice. In this easy-to-read book, Fr. George Elliott accomplishes the seemingly impossible: He clarifies the call to holiness and holds his readers to a high standard for answering it. Fr. Elliott teaches young people to cultivate a habit of prayerful listening so as to discern with clarity the specific ways in which God is calling them to holiness. The result is a useful and inspiring resource for personal discernment—a real gift to families and to the Church!"

—Danielle Bean, Author and Manager of www.catholicmom.com

Nihil Obstat:	Reverend Matthew Kauth, STD
	Censor Deputatus
Imprimatur:	Most Reverend Peter J. Jugis, JCD
	Bishop of Charlotte
	June 29, 2018
	Solemnity of Sts. Peter and Paul

The nihil obstat and imprimatur are official declarations that a book is ffree from doctrinal or moral error. No implication is contained therein that those who grant the nihil obstat or imprimatur agree with the contents, opinions, or statements expressed.

Discernment Do's and Don'ts: A Practical Guide to Vocational Discernment © 2018 Rev. George Elliott

All rights reserved. With the exception of short excerpts used in critical review, no part of this work may be reproduced, transmitted, or stored in any form whatsoever without the prior written permission of the publisher.

Unless otherwise noted, Scripture quotations are from the Revised Standard Version of the Bible—Second Catholic Edition (Ignatius Edition), copyright © 2006 National Council of the Churches of Christ in the United States of America. Used by permission. All rights reserved.

All excerpts from papal homilies, messages, and encyclicals Copyright © Libreria Editrice Vaticana. All rights reserved.

Excerpts from the English translation of the Catechism of the Catholic Church for use in the United States of America © 1994, United States Catholic Conference, Inc.—Libreria Editrice Vaticana. Used with permission.

Excerpts from the English translation of the Compendium Catechism of the Catholic Church for use in the United States of America © 2006, United States Catholic Conference, Inc.—Libreria Editrice Vaticana. Used with permission.

Cover/interior design, and illustrations design by www.davidferrisdesign.com

Library of Congress Control Number: 2018950107

ISBN: 978-1-5051-1017-3

Published in the United States by
TAN Books
PO Box 410487
Charlotte, NC 28241
www.TANBooks.com

Printed in the United States of America

CONTENTS

HOLINESS

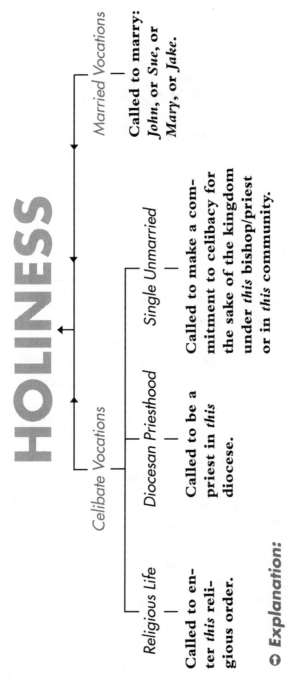

Celibate Vocations			*Married Vocations*
Religious Life	*Diocesan Priesthood*	*Single Unmarried*	
Called to enter *this* religious order.	**Called to be a priest in *this* diocese.**	**Called to make a commitment to celibacy for the sake of the kingdom under *this* bishop/priest or in *this* community.**	**Called to marry: *John*, or *Sue*, or *Mary*, or *Jake*.**

❶ Explanation:

1. Everyone is called to holiness. You are called to your vocation, because it is the best way for you to be holy.
2. Celibate Vocations are objectively higher than married vocations, but they both point toward heaven.
3. Religious Life is objectively higher than Diocesan Priesthood because it takes on the vow of poverty. Diocesan Priesthood is objectively higher than the Single Unmarried life because Diocesan priests take a promise of obedience.

*Note: The actual vocations in this chart are bold. The italicized words are categories of vocations but are not vocations in themselves. Vocations are always particular (i.e., "called to enter this religious order" or "called to marry John", etc.)

◗ Definitions:

Holiness: All the baptized are called to holiness. Holiness consists of being made similar to God through charity.

Celibacy: Celibacy is the state of not being married. Taking a vow of celibacy means that you are going to remain unmarried for the rest of your life.

Celibate Vocations: All vocations that include taking a vow of celibacy are celibate vocations.

Religious Life: Also known as a "religious vocation", is the state of taking vows of poverty, chastity (i.e. celibacy), and obedience. Brothers, monks, sisters, and nuns are all in religious vocations. Most religious orders live in community.

Diocesan Priesthood: These are the priests that you see in most parishes. They take promises of celibacy and obedience. They are attached to a certain area of the world (called a "diocese"), and they fulfill any need that the bishop of that diocese has.

Single Unmarried: Also known as "consecrated single life", is the state of taking a promise of celibacy. Consecrated Singles sometimes live in community, and they sometimes live alone. They also sometimes work in the world, and they sometimes dedicate themselves to prayer away from society.

Married Vocations: The category of vocations that are calls to marry a particular person.

FOREWORD

Trying to find your vocation will be one of the greatest scavenger hunts of your life! The desire to do God's will and ask the bold question, "Lord, what do you want of me?" opens you to an adventure that's unimaginable in its breadth and depth. This adventure will involve questions, sacrifices, illuminations, delays, disappointments, joys, twists and turns, ups and downs. It might take you where you do not want to go or lead you along paths you never anticipated.

When you, as a disciple of Jesus Christ, declare an unconditional surrender to the Lord, you accept an invitation to begin an amazing journey over which you will have no control and within which you will have no bargaining chips. It is a road that will require total trust and vulnerability since it is only this resignation that will allow you to hear God's voice, distinguish it from other voices, and then decide to do whatever God asks of you.

In this way, your discipleship leads to discernment, and authentic discernment will lead to a decision.

For almost six years, I served as the vicar of vocations for the Diocese of Charleston, South Carolina. In that capacity, I saw many young people blessed with insights and consolations into God's will for them. Some said "yes" to the Lord, picked up their cross, and did their best to follow him. Others, however, became frozen through "paralysis by analysis." They were afraid of commitment and missing out on other things. Still others were distracted by pleasure or the allure of worldly delights. In each case in which a "no" was given to God's will, there was a noticeable eclipse of the beatitude of heaven. The perspective of eternity was lost. God's love and care for us was doubted. Happiness was restricted to the things of this world.

And so, in order for us to truly discern God's will, we must live as disciples. This posture means acknowledging that Jesus Christ is Lord, not us. It means accepting that we cannot figure out everything by ourselves and that we need to pray and study the Bible. This way of life calls for the ordering of our passions and the flourishing of virtue. It means we frequent the sacraments as often as possible and seek to deny ourselves so that Jesus Christ's passion, death, and resurrection is re-lived in and through us every day.

Only this radical way of life, through which God becomes our friend, companion, and confidante, will bring us to some level of certainty regarding God's will for us. As we walk with him, we understand his ways, and so desire to dwell within his Divine Providence more perfectly in all our decisions and actions. By living this way, our vocation becomes clear and we're invited to say "yes."

This is not an easy path nor is it one that should be braved alone. The Lord always sends us help. We just have to look for it. Happily, in this year of our Lord 2018, we who wish to do God's will are blessed with this wonderful new book! Without a doubt, Father George Elliott proves himself to be a spiritual master and helpful guide in the process of discipleship and discernment. Father Elliott presents the challenging principles of discernment in a casual, readable, and attractive way. He does not overwhelm with lofty theology but rather applies eternal wisdom in a way *that can help you* know God's will.

Father Elliott is not only a spiritual master but a witness. As a young cadet in the Air Force Academy, he heard the maxim of a good officer: "Service before self." It invigorated him even as it frustrated him. The maxim, so fulfilling to those called to military service, seemed incomplete and lacking in something for him. He asked hard questions. He turned to the sacraments and prayer. He wrestled with his own wants and plans. He sought the Lord's will and wanted to listen to and obey him. This openness of heart helped the future Father Elliott to hear the call of the Lord Jesus. He left the academy, entered the seminary, and, after his time of formation, accepted ordination as a priest of the New Covenant.

This is what discernment looks like and how it concludes. For Father Elliott, it was the holy priesthood. For many, it will be Holy Matrimony. For others, it might be religious life or some other form of consecrated service. And for still others, it could be single for the Lord. In all the above, the goal is not the vocation itself but our love for God and our willingness to do whatever he asks of us.

And so *relax and prepare yourself* for a great read on discernment by a priest who has been there, who has nourished his experience with divine wisdom and a love for the Lord, and who pastorally and generously desires to share these treasures with you!

Father Jeffrey F. Kirby, STD
Author, *Kingdom of Happiness: Living the
Beatitudes in Everyday Life*

PREFACE

"Take heart young people! Christ is calling you and the world awaits you! Remember that the Kingdom of God needs your generous and complete dedication. Do not act like the rich young man, who, invited by Christ, was unable to choose and kept his possessions and his sadness (see Mt 19:22)."[1] With these words, Pope St. John Paul II calls you to enter into a generous and concerted discernment of your vocation.

The decision to enter definitively into a particular vocation is the most important decision of your life. When you choose a vocation, you are making the lifelong decision to dedicate yourself to holiness in a particular way. The importance of this choice can be daunting. Any young person overwhelmed with the responsibility of such a decision needs the support, guidance, and encouragement of those who have gone before. The numerous possibilities can further delay the choice of a vocation due to choice overload. Through this book I intend to provide you—Catholic high school students, college students, and young adults—with the support, guidance, and encouragement necessary to confidently discern and begin the journey towards your vocation.

Many discernment books currently published in the English language either provide the theory behind the process of discernment without giving practical advice on how to go about discerning, or they provide information on how to discern a particular vocation (typically a celibate vocation). Both of those genres are very good and necessary. This book is a *practical* guide on how to discern *any vocation, whether married or celibate.*

I want to make it very clear: I do not want all of my readers to become priests or religious. Many of the people who will read this book are likely called to married life, and, if so, I want them to be married. Likewise, I do not want all of my readers to become husbands or wives, because at least some portion of my readers are likely called to a celibate vocation. The goal of this book is to help young Catholics to enter into the particular vocation to which God is calling them. As a diocesan priest living my vocation, I have found profound peace, joy, and love far beyond anything I could have imagined. I am convinced that peace, joy, and love comes from living the vocation to which God called me, and I want all of my readers to enter into the vocation to which God is calling them so that they can experience that same peace, joy, and love that God has given to me.

xvi

○ *Structure of the Book*

This book is structured according to two principles: 1) Grace perfects nature[2], and 2) the fundamental vocation is the vocation to holiness.[3] This book starts from a recognition that God created us as good. Then it moves to the growth in holiness that perfects that nature. After encouraging the reader to take up the ordinary means of holiness, the book gives some theory but more practical guidance on how to go about discerning a particular vocation.

Each of the chapters includes a mix of practical advice, theory of discernment, and some humor to keep us from taking ourselves too seriously. The chapters are structured so as to give some direction to the work: to encourage the reader to devote the time and energy necessary to discern and, after sufficient clarity has been achieved, to take the next step in the discernment process. Chapter 1, entitled "You," is intended to give readers the confidence necessary to take on the monumental task of discerning their vocations without sloughing off the job by simply complying with someone else's desires. Chapters 2 and 3, entitled "Holiness" and "Prayer," are intended to encourage readers along the path of holiness and provide concrete things they should be doing if they truly take the call to be holy seriously. Chapters 4 to 6, entitled "Time," "Talk," and "Know," deal more directly with the practicalities of discernment. Chapter 7, entitled "Act," is designed to help readers understand what sufficient clarity means and how to go about taking the all-important next step in discernment.

Each chapter starts with a real-life story drawn from my own experience giving spiritual guidance to young adults (names and details have been changed for confidentiality). Then, a number of subheadings clarify the topic at hand, providing some theory of discernment as well as practical ways to go about the discerning step specific to each chapter. Lastly, each chapter has one "Do" and one "Don't" targeting the best practices and common pitfalls of vocational discernment in each of the seven areas treated. Read these Do's and Don'ts frequently in your discernment process. It is important to remind yourself and make sure you are proceeding in the proper fashion to most effectively discern your vocation.

➲ *Theological Foundations*

Among Catholic theologians, there are a variety of theologies and opinions regarding vocations and vocational discernment. The approach that I have taken is one that attempts not to embrace any one thinker or period of Church history but rather to read each of the writers in light of the entire tradition of the Church. My primary sources are the Scriptures, the Fathers of the Church (particularly those who can be loosely categorized as part of the monastic tradition, such as St. Augustine, St. Jerome, St. Benedict, St. John Cassian, etc.), St. Thomas Aquinas, St. Ignatius of Loyola, St. Alphonsus Liguouri, St. Francis de Sales,

St. Thérèse of Lisieux, and Pope St. John Paul II. I also owe much to the outstanding work *Paths of Love* written by Joseph Bolin. The theological foundations of *Discernment Do's and Don'ts* come from years of study of the above-mentioned authors while I was discerning my own vocation and guiding others to do the same. The following brief outline is not meant to be a defense of this book's theological foundations but rather an explanation of certain key concepts to help the reader more clearly understand points made later in the work.

The Idea of Vocation

The foundational and first vocation of every human being is the call to holiness.

> Therefore, in the Church, everyone whether belonging to the hierarchy, or being cared for by it, is called to holiness, according to the saying of the Apostle: "For this is the will of God, your sanctification."[4]

The first choice that you have to make in discerning a vocation is whether you are going to say yes to the call to holiness. To be holy is everyone's vocation, a general vocation of the human race if you will. This decision, if followed until death, will be the difference between going to heaven or not. What is commonly referred to as your particular vocation is the path you are going to take to live out that call to holiness in your life. God creates that path for you, and he created you to follow that path; vocational discernment is the process of coming to know and freely choosing to say yes to the particular path God created for you, the path he created you for. Yes, God created you to accomplish some task for him during your time on earth. A powerful thought!

Some people claim that if one does not enter into one's true God-given vocation, one cannot be saved or can be saved only with difficulty. I disagree with that theory. It would be a sin knowingly not to choose the vocation to which God is calling you, but that does not mean that the gates of heaven are closed to someone who has done so. God's mercy is always available, and even after sinful or merely mistaken decisions, conversion is possible, holiness is possible, and salvation is possible. As evidenced by the many holy souls who entered into married life in their youth without proper discernment and only later, when they began to strive for holiness, recognized that they were likely called to priesthood or religious life, responding properly to one's vocation does not seem to be necessary for salvation.

The question can be asked: if properly discerning your vocation is not necessary for salvation, what's the point of discerning? Living the vocation that God created for you is the quickest and easiest path to holiness. It is the path that will bring you the most joy, peace, love, and holiness. Not choosing that path will make living a holy life more difficult, but it doesn't mean that you can't get to heaven. An example is the man and woman who married without proper discernment. The disagreements in the marriage escalated to the point that they had to separate. Now they are required to live chastely as separated persons. Can they be saved? Yes. Will their life and path to salvation be more difficult than if they had properly discerned their vocation? Yes.

Lastly, it is important to note that nobody is called to marriage in general, and nobody is called to celibacy in general.[5] Vocations are always particular. In the words of Pope St. John Paul II, "A vocation always means some principal direction of love of a particular man or woman."[6] Therefore, a vocation is not a call to a generality but rather to a particular: "I am called to marry John," or, "I am called to live celibacy in this community." Trying to discern generalities apart from the particulars can cause a villainizing or idealizing of a particular vocation, which would unduly block or skew the discernment process. More on this topic will be explained in later chapters.

Objectively Better Vocations and Subjectively Better Vocations

One of two major thoughts dominate Catholics' view of the comparison between vocations to the religious life, the other celibate vocations, and married life. On one extreme are the people who consider those living religious life to be the "real Catholics," while married people are second class citizens. They see married people as somehow "lesser than" people living celibacy, and they consider that married people are not called to real holiness. That opinion is completely wrong. On the opposite extreme are the people that consider all vocations absolutely equal in the eyes of God or perhaps even that there is something odd about celibate vocations. (Although, interestingly enough, their scorn for celibacy seems often restricted to Catholics. Buddhist monks and nuns who are celibate seem immune from such criticism.) The most characteristic people in this group are those who push for married priests. They see celibacy as something which is difficult, and they see no fruit in it. Therefore, they think celibacy should be abandoned. This idea is also completely wrong.

When Christ tells the young man who wishes to be perfect to sell his possessions and come follow him, he is laying out the vows of poverty and obedience as the way of the "perfect."[7] Therefore, the vows of poverty and obedience are, in fact, the objectively highest (i.e., objectively "perfect") vocation. The New Testament lays out the superiority of celibacy for the sake of the kingdom (see Lk 18:29–30; Mt 19:11–12) and how it furnishes man with an undivided heart for the Lord (see 1 Cor 7:33–35). The Fathers of the Church[8] and the saints through the centuries[9] also have strongly held that poverty and obedience are the way of perfection and the celibate life is a higher vocation than married life. In the Scriptures and in the Tradition of the Church, there is a clear hierarchy of vocations: vocations which embrace vows of chastity, poverty, and obedience are the highest, other celibate vocations are below them, and married life is below any celibate vocation. However, the existence of a hierarchy doesn't mean that the people living in a certain vocation are better or worse than others, or that they are called to a lesser or greater holiness.

If this hierarchy is oversimplified and misunderstood, it can lead to conclusions such as: "marriage is the worst vocation," "marriage is only for those who can't handle celibacy," or "celibacy is for people who want to be saints, and marriage is for the rest of us." Pope St. John Paul II,[10] drawing on the thought of the Fathers of the Church,[11] saints throughout the centuries,[12] and the Second Vatican Council,[13] responded to those conclusions by affirming that marriage is a legitimate and great vocation, a vocation in its own right, and a vocation that is intended to lead to sainthood. The proper understanding is not that marriage is the worst vocation but rather that marriage is a very high vocation, and celibate vocations are higher; marriage is a vocation in its own right and requires its own kind of chastity; and marriage is a way to live out one's call to holiness, not a way to avoid the struggle for holiness. There is nothing evil or bad about marriage. It was created by God from the beginning of the world and was elevated to a sacrament by Jesus Christ. To enter into marriage is good and holy.

Therefore, when looking at vocations, it is not a matter of choosing between a good vocation and a bad vocation but rather between good vocations and better vocations, but always with the determination of discovering the right vocation for you—the vocation that God is calling you to. You must always consider your subjective situation to see which of these good things is best for you. To explain the terms I am using: "subjectively better" means "better for me," whereas "objectively better" means "better in itself without applying it to any particular person or circumstance." A thing which is objectively evil cannot be subjectively better for someone than a thing which is objectively good.

However, in vocations we are not dealing with good vocations and bad vocations—that is, good and evil choices— we are dealing with all good vocations. Therefore, one vocation

xxi

which is objectively better may not be subjectively better for a given person due to a variety of different circumstances. Someone who openly accepts the objective superiority of the vows of poverty, chastity, and obedience could still choose marriage as subjectively better for them for a variety of reasons. In the words of St. Thomas Aquinas, "Though it may be said in general that for an individual man it is better to practice continence than to enter into marriage, nothing prevents marriage from being better for a particular person."[14]

Therefore, when discerning vocations, the benefit of the doubt should be given to the objectively better or higher vocations (vows of poverty, chastity, and obedience or other celibate vocations), but that does not mean that everyone will be called to them. This "benefit of the doubt" will require a significant shift in how the majority of people think about vocations. Most people think about married life first and only secondarily consider celibate vocations. In fact, most people will continue down the road to marriage until they are pulled in an extraordinary way toward celibacy (sad to say, I once was included in that group of people). However, St. Ignatius, the master of discernment of spirits, states in his Directory that more evident signs are required in order to conclude that God is calling someone to marriage than to conclude that God is calling them to embrace the evangelical counsels.[15] These "more evident signs" do not have to be supernatural phenomena; they can be just good, solid reasons that come from sound theology and experience with each of the vocations, evidence that can bring one reasonably to conclude that the subjectively better vocation for them is a married vocation.

For Men: Celibacy and Priesthood

I cannot count how many times I have asked a young man in spiritual direction, "Have you considered a celibate vocation?" and they responded to me, "I discerned the priesthood awhile back, and it just didn't seem like it was for me." I never asked them

about the priesthood. I asked about a celibate vocation. Due to
the shortage of priests in the United States at this time, celibate
vocations are almost never spoken of separate from the priesthood.
Therefore, many Catholics confuse the idea of priesthood and
male celibate vocations, yet they are two very distinct vocations. St.
Paul encourages all the baptized to celibacy (see 1 Cor 7:33–35),
but when Jesus chooses his priests, he calls them by name (see Mt
4:18–22; Mk 1:16–34; Lk 5:1–11). The call to the priesthood is a
particular call that is given to celibate men in the Roman Church.
It requires a certain "positive call" as opposed to the general call of
all of the baptized to the celibate vocations. Practically speaking,
that means that fewer proofs are needed for a man to be certain
that he is called to a celibate vocation than are needed to prove
that he is called to the priesthood. For those particular proofs
for whether one is called to the priesthood, see any of the many
priestly discernment books in publication. Particularly useful is *To
Save a Thousand Souls* by Fr. Brett Brannen.

Even though the call to celibacy and the call to the priesthood   xxiii
are two distinct calls, it is particularly fitting that the Roman
Catholic Church, in her wisdom, chooses to ordain celibate men
to the priesthood. The first reason that celibate priests are most
fitting is the priest "looks to [Christ] directly as his model and
supreme ideal."[16] Jesus Christ was not married. The priest should
be like Jesus Christ. Therefore, priests should not be married. Also,
Jesus Christ gave great dignity to marriage: he raised it to the
level of a sacrament. But Jesus was the mediator of a new and
eternal covenant (see Heb 8:6) and "has also opened a new way,
in which the human creature adheres wholly and directly to the
Lord, and is concerned only with Him and with His affairs; thus,
he manifests in a clearer and more complete way the profoundly
transforming reality of the New Testament."[17]

Jesus's celibacy wasn't just a coincidence. His celibacy was at
the core of what he came to earth to do: form a new covenant
between God and man. The priest continues the mission of Jesus
Christ on earth. Therefore, he too should embrace that core aspect

of celibacy to safeguard the covenant between God and man. Jesus's relationship with the Church is also very significant and fraught with meaning for priestly celibacy. Jesus offered himself entirely for the sake of his bride, the Church. The priest also should be completely free to offer himself with Jesus Christ, his model, for the sake of the Church. In the words of St. John Paul II, "The Church, as the Spouse of Jesus Christ, wishes to be loved by the priest in the total and exclusive manner in which Jesus Christ her Head and Spouse loved her. Priestly celibacy, then, is the gift of self *in* and *with* Christ *to* his Church and expresses the priest's service to the Church in and with the Lord."[18]

Lastly, everything about a priest should point to heaven. In Lk 20:34–36 Jesus says, "The sons of this age marry and are given in marriage; but those who are accounted worthy to attain to that age and to the resurrection from the dead neither marry nor are given in marriage, for they cannot die anymore, because they are equal to angels and are sons of God, being sons of the resurrection." People in heaven are not married, so when the priest is celibate, he is imitating the saints in heaven. Priestly celibacy preaches to the world that this world is not the end. It is like a sign saying that our time on this earth is given to us to get to heaven.

I can say from my own experience that living my life as a celibate priest has brought me more joy and happiness than I ever thought was possible. If someone were to tell me that I could be married, I would reply with a polite, "Thanks, but no thanks!" I am so convinced of the richness of the love that I share with Jesus Christ because I have an undivided heart for him. Because I am celibate, I am able to pour forth upon everyone I meet the life and love that Christ pours out on me. That does not mean that I do not have bad days or that I do not struggle with temptation at times. Everyone has bad days, and even Jesus was tempted. However, I am very happy as a celibate priest, and I thank God for the Church's practice of ordaining celibate men to the priesthood. I must admit that if the Church had not required celibacy to be ordained a priest, I likely would not have taken a serious look at celibacy. I would have simply gotten married and not thought twice about it. I cannot thank Our Lord enough for bringing me to the vocation of *celibate* priesthood!

Types of Vocations

In the period leading up to, during, and following the Second Vatican Council, the Church broadened the traditional understanding of vocational paths to include a wide variety of states, associations, congregations, and orders. While this variety gives a great wealth to the Church, it complicates the life of an author writing about vocations. In this book, I will generally list only three vocational categories: religious life, priesthood, and married life. I do not intend to exclude any of the other possible vocations, but for brevity's sake will only list those three. While reading, please include any of the other vocations sanctioned by Holy Mother Church in your understanding and application of the text.

CHAPTER 1

YOU

⊙ *Anne*

Anne was a junior in high school and had fallen head over heels in love with Jake. He was handsome, funny, popular, and slightly mysterious. Anne was in a few classes with Jake and had a good time with him whenever they talked, but he didn't seem interested in dating her. The difficulty as Anne saw it was that Jake was part of the skater crowd, and, while Anne was by no means a goody-goody, she was certainly not a skater. There was no way that Jake was going to date a girl outside of the skater clique. Without even noticing it herself, Anne slowly started wearing darker makeup and hanging out with the other girls in the skater crowd. She began to listen to different music and started to wonder if her parents would let her get a few more ear piercings. Her cadence of speech changed, and she laughed as she told me that one day while flipping through the channels, she decided to watch the X Games. She began even to change her personality. She would say and do things that she knew weren't really "her," but she was so consumed by the desire to get Jake's attention that she would just forget about them—they weren't sins after all—and count them as worth it if they got his attention.

After several weeks, she was added to a few of the skater crowd's group chats, Jake started to send her messages, and some

1

of the girls invited her to hang out. After becoming more and more part of the clique, Jake eventually invited her to go out with him, and they hit it off. The moment had arrived! Jake was finally hers!

Anne and Jake dated for several months, and while the euphoria of dating the guy that she had been interested in for months kept her distracted at first, she eventually began to wake up to what was going on inside her. She didn't really like the other girls in the skater clique. The music she started listening to gave her a headache. She didn't actually know how to skate (and she was too afraid to learn). So when they went to the park, all she did was stand around and watch. Jake's jokes were really just the same ones that all of the other skater guys made. Anne had nothing in common with Jake. She realized that she didn't really like Jake, and she didn't really like the person she had become. She felt like she was always acting to impress people that she didn't understand and that she didn't really enjoy being around. By the end of the school year, Jake and Anne broke up and were both happier for it. Anne began to hang out with her old friends again, returned to her old self, graduated from high school the following year, left for college, and now, after graduating, is engaged to a guy whose attention she got without acting like someone other than herself!

Though we may not realize it, even such early dating experiences can and should be a part of the vocational discernment process. While Anne was in the earliest stages of vocational discernment with Jake, she made a mistake that many people do in this process. She failed to recognize three things: first, God created her the way she is; second, God has a plan for her; and, finally, acting unlike her true self was only going to skew the discernment process, even if she did not realize she was discerning anything at all while she was dating Jake.

⊃ What Do "You" Have to Do With Vocational Discernment?

God Made You, and He Doesn't Make Mistakes

Johann von Goethe said, "If God had wanted me otherwise, he would have created me otherwise." This could be taken as an arrogant statement, but it could also be considered a profound reflection. God did not make a mistake when he created you or any other person. If he had wanted you to be different, he would have created you differently. That means God wants you to be you with all of your personality traits, your strengths, your weaknesses, and your looks (or lack thereof!) to fulfill the plan that he has laid out for you, "for we are his workmanship, created in Christ Jesus for good works, which God prepared beforehand, that we should walk in them" (Eph 2:10). But be careful. This notion does not mean that you should just casually accept your character flaws without any effort to improve them or to acquire the opposing virtues.

3

This concept can be applied or understood in a variety of ways. First, it means that if you are not at least somewhat comfortable with who you are, you aren't going to be able to discern God's vocation for you. Our first calling, even before the call to holiness, is the call to be who and what God created us to be. If you are rejecting yourself as God created you, and there is "a certain *calling* into existence through creation,"[19] then you are already rejecting your first vocation from God who is calling you to be you.

King David is an excellent example for us. He was not like his older brothers, tall and striking and strong, but the Lord chose David for the task at hand because "the LORD sees not as man sees; man looks on the outward appearance, but the LORD looks on the heart" (1 Sm 16:7). If David had not been so small, Goliath would not have lowered his shield and laughed so that David could strike him with the rock from his sling. If David had not had years of practice with the harp while watching the sheep, he would not have been so favored by King Saul early on. If David had not lived in the wilderness for years, he would not have survived in the wilderness while fleeing from Saul. And yet who would have thought that being utterly unintimidating, knowing how to play the harp, and having wilderness survival skills would have been essential to become the great king of the Israelites? If Goliath had not lowered his shield to laugh at David, there no longer would have been a Kingdom of Israel. If David's musical talent had not pleased King Saul, he never would have been permitted into the inner circle of the king. If he had not survived in the wilderness while King Saul was pursuing him, he would not have lived to see the day of his coronation. All of these "little" characteristics of David were indispensable for him to fulfill the will of God. David did not wish that he was like his brothers. He even rejected the sword and shield forced on him by the other Israelites before facing Goliath (see 1 Sm 17:39). He accepted himself as he was—as God made him—and God used him, with all of his characteristics, to fulfill his plan.

4

Another realization that emerges from the understanding that God created you the way you are is that your personality traits (which have to be distinguished from personality flaws!) will be good for your vocation: "For everything created by God is good, and nothing is to be rejected" (1 Tm 4:4). If you are extroverted, then God will use that in your vocation. If you are quiet, then God will use that in your vocation. If you are short, if you are tall, if you are reserved, if you are thoughtful, if you move quickly, if you reflect often, if you are smart (or the contrary) . . . whatever characteristics God gave you, he will use in the fulfillment of his plan for you. When we recognize this, and let it soak in, we almost naturally burst out with the Psalmist:

> I praise you, for I am wondrously made.
> Wonderful are your works!

You know me right well;
my frame was not hidden from you,
when I was being made in secret,
intricately wrought in the depths of the
earth.
Your eyes beheld my unformed substance;
in your book were written, every one of
them,
the days that were formed for me,
when as yet there was none of them. (Ps
139:14–16)

God created you "wondrously" and formed your "days." He created you well and has a plan for you specifically. That plan will carry you to true freedom, because in God's plan you will be able to flourish while being yourself: "where the Spirit of the Lord is, there is freedom." There is no personality trait that has to be suppressed or forgotten to live your vocation. You will be able to be yourself and become a saint in the vocation that God has planned for you. In the words of St. Catherine of Siena, "Be who God meant you to be and you will set the world on fire."[20]

God Has a Plan for You, and It's Better Than Your Plan for You

How often have you reflected on the fact that God created a plan specifically for you? From the beginning of time he has intended you to exist and to receive his loving care. He chose to create you in this time, in this country, in this family, with these challenges, with these joys, because he sees that those circumstances will offer you the chance to live a joy-filled and fulfilling life and, most importantly, to become a great saint. He says to every one of us, "For I know the plans I have for you, . . . plans for welfare and not for evil, to give you a future and a hope," (Jer 29:11) and, "Are not two sparrows sold for a penny? And not one of them will fall to the ground without your Father's will. But even the hairs of your head are all numbered. Fear not, therefore; you are of more value than many sparrows" (Mt 10:29–31). These two passages proclaim clearly that God has a plan for you. It is the best plan possible, and he has it worked out even in the details.

This means two things for every human: 1) God has a plan for your life, and it's better than your plans. 2) It's your job to say yes to God in the overarching plan and in each of the details.

In soccer, a principle of on-field communication is that you listen to the teammate with the best view of the field. That person is usually the goalkeeper. While it may seem instinctual to listen to the nearby teammate calling "pass!", they may not see the opponent closing in behind them. The goalie standing all the way at the end of the field, who knows the strengths and weaknesses of each player, has the full view of the field and can give the best instructions to the rest of the team. God is like the cosmological goalkeeper in the soccer game of salvation. He knows the strengths and weaknesses of each player because he created every one of them, and he sees the entire playing field because he knows all things at all times. Even though we may think that a certain decision or plan for our life is the best, we may not see that obstacle or opportunity closing in behind us. God knows the "field," and his plan is the best one possible.

God not only knows the best vocation for you but also has the best plan for you to arrive at that vocation. God created you and loves you. If God created you, then he knows what will make you happy. If God loves you, then he wants you to be happy. Therefore, doing what God wants you to do is the best and easiest way to be happy. God knows not only the end result that will make you happy but also the best way to get to that end result. This logic applies not only in your general vocation but also in each and every step that leads you to your vocation. It can be applied to every moment of your life and every decision you make.

Returning to the analogy of the soccer game, the player with the ball may know that his purpose (read "vocation") is to shoot the ball at the goal, but from where he is standing, he only has a mediocre shot on the goal. The player with the full view of the field knows that it would be better to cross the ball rather than take a shot from that location, because the player across the field has a wide-open shot. Therefore, even in a little detail about how or when to make a shot on the goal, it is best to listen to the player with the better view of the field.

The same applies to vocational discernment. God's call does not simply give us an end goal and leave us to deal with figuring out how to get there, "He leads [us] in paths of righteousness" (Ps 23:3). He knows the details of our lives and the circumstances surrounding us. He can foresee difficulties and pitfalls that we never would have been able to predict. He can also foresee joys and blessings that we never would have found had we not followed the path laid out by him. It requires great trust in God to allow him to lead you step by step, but it is well worth it. Sometimes he will take longer than you wanted; sometimes he will move faster than you wanted; sometimes he will take you down a path that you would prefer not to travel; but it will always be the best path and the one that will lead you to the greatest happiness, peace, and sanctity.

God Is Calling You

Do you remember the telephone game? The game that you would play as a little kid when one person would come up with a word or phrase and would whisper that word or phrase into one person's ear, then that person would whisper it into another person's ear, and so on until you got to the end of the group? The last person would then say out loud the word or phrase that they heard, and inevitably all of the kids giggle because the word or phrase said out loud sounded nothing like the word or phrase that the first person said. While the telephone game is a silly children's game, it contains an important lesson: passing a message through other people is a terrible way to communicate. If the person for whom the message is intended can be reached directly, it's best to just tell them directly. God understands the same thing. The telephone game doesn't work. When God is calling someone to a particular vocation, he communicates that call to the person directly.

Problems often arise in a young person's discernment process when they are pressured by another person to enter into a certain vocation: a mother may want her son to become a priest, a father may want his daughter to marry a certain man, a friend or group of friends may pressure a person to enter or not to enter a given religious community. While a mentor who knows you well can be a great guide in understanding God's call, God's call is not communicated by the pressures or preferences of other human beings. God is calling you, not them. If he wants you to do something, he'll communicate that to you.

A great example of this is the calling of Samuel. God called directly to Samuel four times, "Samuel! Samuel!" (1 Sm 3:4; see also 1 Sm 3:6, 3:8, 3:10). But Samuel "did not yet know the LORD, and the word of the LORD had not yet been revealed to him" (1 Sm 3:7), so he needed Eli's guidance to understand the call that he was experiencing: "Go, lie down; and if he calls you, you shall say, 'Speak, LORD, for your servant hears'" (1 Sm 3:9). And even though Samuel turned to Eli for guidance, God then communicated directly with Samuel: "And Samuel said, 'Speak, for your servant hears.' Then the LORD said to Samuel, 'Behold, I am about to do a thing in Israel . . .'" (1 Sm 3:10–11).

God will communicate his will for you to you. As Pope St. John Paul II says, "The calling of man first finds its source in God: in man's mind and in the choice that God himself makes and which man needs to read in his own heart."[21] Your vocation comes from God, and you will recognize that vocation in your mind and in your heart. Other people can help you significantly in understanding how to go about discerning, they can help you understand the different vocations that you may be called to, and they can help you sort through the movements of God in your heart, but they cannot tell you exactly what your vocation is.

These other people are like doctors interpreting the symptoms of a person's illness. You can tell them all of the symptoms that you are experiencing, and they can help you interpret those symptoms, but they can't dictate or pressure you into having certain symptoms. How ridiculous would it be for a doctor to come in and tell the patient what the patient's symptoms are?

Similarly, while we all may put on a sweater to keep our mothers happy when they are convinced that we feel cold (even though they are really just projecting their feeling chilly onto us), choosing a certain vocation because your mother pressured you to do so is like choosing to put on a sweater for the rest of your life that has a personality, will raise your kids, is fairly expensive, and which your mother will only see at Thanksgiving and Christmas. It's absolute insanity!

◌ Do's and Don'ts

The two most common mistakes in vocational discernment in regard to "You" are that people often act unlike themselves when they are discerning, which completely skews the discernment process, or they reject or accept a certain vocation in order to make someone else happy.

Do: Be Yourself When You Are Discerning a Vocation

"Let us be what we are and be that well," says St. Francis de Sales.[22] God knows you intimately, and he knows everyone around you intimately. His plan for you and for everyone else makes all of the personality strengths and weaknesses of the world around you fit for the accomplishment of his plan. Think of yourself as a puzzle piece in the great puzzle of salvation history. God cut you to fit into a certain place in the puzzle, so if you start forming yourself into some other shape than you really are, you will no longer fit in the puzzle. When you are discerning how you fit into the big puzzle of life, you won't find your right place if you deform yourself every time you try out a spot.

What happens if someone does deform themselves? Luckily, God is really good at puzzles and can still make a beautiful image out of dysfunctional puzzle pieces. God writes straight with crooked lines or, perhaps more fittingly, makes beautiful puzzles with broken pieces. But those distorted puzzle pieces will forever be in that distorted position and will over time feel the pain and stress due to being in the wrong spot.

Don't: Choose a Vocation to Make Somebody Else Happy

Your vocation is your vocation. God will communicate his will for you to you, and once you enter into a vocation, you are the one living it out for the rest of your life. It doesn't matter how happy your mom will be that you became a priest. It doesn't matter how happy your friends will be that you married that girl. It doesn't matter how sad your siblings will be that you entered that religious order. If you aren't called to that vocation, don't do it! We don't need any more unhappy priests, religious, or families in the world. If you enter into a vocation to make someone else happy, you are committing a sin against a multitude of people. If you were called to a celibate vocation but entered married life, think of all of the people that you could have served, to say nothing of the injustice done to your spouse. If you were called to married life but entered a celibate vocation, think of the boyfriend or girlfriend you left behind: Who will be his wife? Who will be her husband? And consider the difficulties you may experience with celibacy if your true calling was to marriage.

This has been a difficulty for centuries, and the Moral Doctor of the Church, St. Alphonsus Liguori, in his work directed to confessors, specifically references the pressures that family members can put on someone to enter into a particular vocation.

He gives a great summary of how we should approach pressures to enter a given vocation:

> Let the confessor test well the vocation of his penitent, asking whether the penitent has some obstacle to it, due to incapacity, poor health, or the need of his parents. And let him especially weigh his purpose, to see if it is right, i.e., in order to unite himself more closely to God, or to amend the falls of his previous life, or to avoid the dangers of the world. But if the primary end is worldly—in order to lead a more agreeable life, or to free himself from relatives of an unfeeling character, or *to please his parents, who push him to this*—let him beware of permitting him to enter religious life. For in that case, it is not a true vocation, and entering in this way, without a true vocation, will have a bad outcome. But if the end is good, and no obstacle is present, then neither the confessor, nor anyone else, as St. Thomas teaches, (Quodlib. 3, art. 14), should or can without grave fault impede him, or attempt to dissuade him from the vocation."[23]

If you don't have a well-founded reason not to enter a certain vocation that you personally feel called to enter, then go in that direction. Do not worry yourself about what other people will think or say. If you are not acting rashly, and you are striving to do God's will, then he will take care of everyone else around you. Doing God's will for you is the best thing for you and for everyone else in your life.

✪ Discussion/Reflection Questions

- How often do you think about how God intentionally made you to be who you are?

11

- When you think about your vocation, do you think about yourself being in that vocation? Or do you think about some other version of yourself being in that vocation?

- Do you feel pressured by anyone to enter into a particular vocation?

- Have you ever acted not as yourself to try to make a vocation work (whether to marry someone or to enter into a celibate vocation)?

- Name some of your personality traits.

- What are some areas of your personality (i.e., personality flaws) that could use conversion?

CHAPTER 2

HOLINESS

○ Mark

While in the seminary, seminarians are assigned to help out at nearby parishes throughout the year. It gives the seminarians an opportunity to do pastoral work and gives the parishes a little extra help. In my first parish assignment as a seminarian, there was a man named Mark.

13

Mark was the image of true manhood. He was a hardworking, devout, intelligent, fun, and normal guy. He loved the Church, and he loved his wife. All of his children were out of the house by the time I got to know him, but when they came in to visit, you could tell that he had been a good father by the devotion that they showed to him. He had served twenty years in the Marines and, despite being about fifty years old, was still as fit as he had been when he was twenty. After serving in the Marines, he moved to Philadelphia and started his own small business. It didn't make him rich, but it gave him the flexibility to do what he enjoyed. He spent much of his time serving at the church: he taught Faith Formation with his wife, he led a men's Bible study, and he was one of the leaders in the St. Vincent de Paul Society. Everybody in the area, Catholics and non-Catholics alike, respected Mark.

Toward the end of the year, Mark came out of the church after Mass and started walking straight towards me. He looked serious, and because he was a fairly large man, I must admit I was a bit intimidated at first! But as he approached, I realized he had tears in his eyes. I couldn't imagine what would make this big, tough image of the perfect man tear up.

He came up to me and said, "I've been meaning to tell you: never give up on your vocation. I went to the seminary for six months, but I struggled with impurity, and instead of fighting against it, I just gave up, left the seminary, and got married. I know I could have overcome it, but I just didn't want to fight it. It was the worst decision of my life. There isn't a day that goes by that I don't think of all the souls that could have been helped by me persevering, and it breaks my heart. Don't give up!" He then wrapped his huge arms around me, gave me a hug, and briskly walked out of the church.

I stood there stunned. I never would have thought that this man for whom I, and so many other people, had so much respect could be going through such internal suffering about a vocational decision he had made in his youth. And yet he said it clearly, "There isn't a day that goes by that I don't think of all the souls that I could have helped had I followed God's will, and it breaks my heart."

That brief moment with Mark made a deep impression on me. Mark taught me that just because you may be struggling with a certain sin, that doesn't mean you aren't called to a certain vocation. We need to do everything we can to get sin out of our lives to live any vocation well, whether married or celibate. While we can't say whether God would have called Mark to persevere until the end of the seminary and to be ordained a priest, Mark's story shows that avoiding a vocation because of vice is not how God intends us to discern his call.

○ What Does Holiness Have to Do With Vocational Discernment?

Our First Vocation as Baptized Christians Is the Vocation to Holiness

"All the faithful, whatever their condition or state—though each in his own way—are called by the Lord to that perfection of sanctity by which the Father himself is perfect."[24] The Second Vatican Council in its document Lumen Gentium makes it clear, "All the faithful . . . are called by the Lord to that perfection of sanctity." It doesn't say, "Priests and religious are called to perfect sanctity, but everyone else is called to mediocrity." It doesn't say, "Parents have to be patient so they can raise their kids well, but priests and religious can be impatient." And it doesn't say, "Priests and religious need the virtue of chastity, but married people don't." It says that everyone has to be holy. Period.

This idea that we all have to be holy isn't anything new. The Second Vatican Council simply called for a renewed emphasis on living it out. From the beginning of the Church, Christians understood well their call to holiness. Even before Christ, God called his people to be holy: "Say to all the congregation of the sons of Israel, You shall be holy; for I the LORD your God am holy" (Lv 19:2). And after Christ ascended into heaven, Paul called his fellow Christians "saints" in almost every one of his letters (see Rm 1:7; 1 Cor 6:1; 2 Cor 1:1; Eph 1:1; Phil 1:1; 1 Thes 3:13; 2 Thes 1:10; 1 Tm 5:10; Phlm 1:5; Heb 6:10), and he recognized that sanctity was not just a state of being but a real calling of all Christians, we "who are called to be saints" (Rm 1:7; see also 1 Cor 1:2).

The word *saint* comes from the Latin word *sanctus*, which is the Latin term for "holy." Think of how we sing, "Sanctus, sanctus, sanctus," or, "Holy, holy, holy," in Mass depending on whether the Mass parts are in Latin or English. Therefore, to be holy is to be a saint, and to be a saint is to be holy. It's the same thing. The

15

call to holiness is the call to sainthood, and as the Second Vatican Council says, that call is directed to every single Christian, you included. This call to sainthood doesn't mean that God expects us to spend all our time levitating in ecstasy or carrying out extreme penances. God does have extraordinary vocations in store for some people, but these extraordinary lives are not required for holiness.

As the Compendium of the Catechism states, "[Holiness] is the fullness of Christian life and the perfection of charity."[25] To be holy means to live God's commandments and to be virtuous so that we can love as God loves. (Jn 13:34: "A new commandment I give to you, that you love one another; even as I have loved you.") It means to love God and neighbor wherever God has placed you at this moment. Holiness can and should be lived out doing the normal things of life. If you are a student, you live holiness by doing your studies for love of God, by being a loving friend, a loving son or daughter, a loving sibling. If you are working, you can do your work with excellence for the glory of God and the salvation of souls with a heart full of love. You can be a source of love in your workplace. You can use part of your income to support the Church and other charitable groups. In whatever stage in life you may find yourself now, God is calling you to be holy by loving right there where you are.

Do not be afraid to strive for real sainthood now. It will not make you weird or abnormal. In fact, it will make you even more normal. St. Josemaria Escriva in *Furrow* says it well, "Saints, abnormal? . . . The time has come to do away with that prejudice,"[26] and "when we work wholly and exclusively for the glory of God, we do everything with naturalness."[27] The saints are the most natural and are most themselves because they are most free. They are not held back by the bonds of sin and vice, and they consequently have a holy naturalness about them.

16

You Need Holiness to Live Any Vocation Well, So Start Working On It Now!

Would you be interested in marrying someone who didn't love? Hopefully not! Anyone in their right mind wants a loving spouse and a loving father or mother for their future children. Similarly, would it make any sense for someone to say, "I decided I just didn't want to love, so I got married"? Not at all! Marriage is a sacrament of mutual love. Without true and authentic love, which does not always originate as some great romantic "love" out of the movies, married life would be an enormous burden.

Or again, would it make any sense for someone to become a priest or religious if they didn't want to be holy? No! Celibate vocations are specifically dedicated so that those who are living celibacy can have an undivided heart to love Christ. A priest or religious who is not striving for holiness would be a scandal to all of the people he meets and would be ineffective in his work of evangelization.

Experience shows us that it is impossible to love as God calls us to love without all of the virtues working together to support that crowning virtue of charity.[28] Therefore, to live out this call to holiness, we have to struggle against our vices and work day in and day out to grow in virtue.

The most important virtues needed to live a vocation well are the theological virtues of faith, hope, and charity. Every vocation, whatever it is, requires the person to love heroically and to love as Christ loved (see Jn 13:34). Without a firm faith founded on the loving plan of the Father specifically for you, you will not have the grounding to be able to love as is required in your vocation. Without a firm hope in eternal life, you will lose the motivation to love when Christ asks you to "take up [your] cross and follow me" (Mt 16:24) and to truly give of yourself in your vocation. Lastly, without that divine charity coursing through your soul, you will turn from the cross and will not love as you should whenever Christ asks you to die to yourself in imitation of him:

17

"Greater love has no man than this, that a man lay down his life for his friends" (Jn 15:13).

To give an example, when a husband and father comes home after a long day at work, his vocation is going to ask him to love heroically. His boss was rude to him all day, he has a splitting headache, and the only thing he wants to do is to sit down by himself in silence and do nothing. But when he walks through the door, his kids are going to come running to him wanting him to pick them up. They're going to have in their hands the loudest toy in the world that his mother-in-law gave them. They are going to want all of his attention and to show him the work they did at school, the pictures they painted in the afternoon, and the worm that they caught in the yard right before he arrived. And that's not all. His wife is going to want to talk to him because she is distraught that little Tommy got in trouble at school, Isaac refused to eat his lunch, Cecilia got paint all over her dress, and Clara threw up on the sofa. He is going to have to die to himself and draw on his faith in the love of God and the hope in eternity to be able to love as a father and a husband at that moment, and truly love his family as Christ loves them. Without the theological virtues alive in his soul, he will be unable to respond to the demands of his vocation in that instant.

To grow in the theological virtues of faith, hope, and love, we need sanctifying grace, which we receive in the sacraments. Therefore, to continue to grow in these virtues, and to prepare ourselves to live our vocation well, we should make frequent use of the sacraments, specifically Penance and Communion. In the sacrament of Penance, we receive the forgiveness of our sins, which are like barriers that we have built between ourselves and God, and in Communion, we receive Christ himself, the source and summit of the Christian life. Drinking from the font of the theological virtues, we draw closer to Christ and grow in faith, hope, and charity.

Beyond the theological virtues, we also need the moral virtues to live any vocation well. The moral virtues are prudence, justice, fortitude, temperance, chastity, sobriety, humility, meekness, clemency, studiousness, perseverance, magnanimity, piety, truthfulness, and gratitude to name a few. If you aren't entirely sure what one of those virtues is, look it up or ask someone who knows the Faith well to explain it to you.

These virtues are required to live any vocation well. For example, the patience of the exhausted father who comes home after a hard day's work to an overzealous gaggle of kids is the same patience of the priest who, after four hours of confessions, has to deal with interpersonal disputes between volunteers. The prudence of a mother who has to know how to discipline her son who misbehaved is the same prudence required of a religious superior who has to know how to discipline the sister in her community who can't seem to get anything right. The chastity of the married man requires him to relate with all of the women in the world, except for one woman, in the exact same way a religious brother would relate with those same women. What is more, even the married man's relationship with his wife still has to be regulated by chastity![29] Every single vocation requires great virtue, and that virtue has to be practiced, learned, and acquired through the pursuit of holiness.

How do you grow in the moral virtues? The quote by St. Francis de Sales on love can be applied to all of the virtues: "You learn to speak by speaking, to study by studying, to run by running, to work by working, and just so, you learn to love by loving. All those who think to learn in any other way deceive themselves."[30] You grow in the virtues by practicing them, by intentionally living them out. Virtues are defined as good habits. Think of what a virtuous person would do in your situation and do that. As you continue to do the virtuous thing, you will become a virtuous person, and then virtue will become like a second nature.[31]

Would You Tell Anyone Your Will If They Disregarded It Most of the Time?

If you had a long history with a person who continually didn't do what you asked, would you bother telling them what you want? No. It would be a waste of your breath. If they haven't listened to you in the last fifteen years, and they haven't shown any sign of wanting to change, why would they start listening now? It would be crazy to think that they are all of a sudden going to change and do what you ask.

God, however, continues to call us; will we hear him? God has clearly revealed to us what he wants: "This is the will of God, your sanctification" (1 Thes 4:3–4). The Church teaches that sin is contrary to our sanctification and is an offense against the will of God.[32] When we sin, we disregard what God has asked of us and do the opposite of what he wants. Therefore, it's completely reasonable that if our lives are dominated by sin, we'll be too blinded by sin to see or hear what he is telling us. In the words of the prophet Isaiah, "But your iniquities have made a separation between you and your God" (Is 59:2).

So before you really start concerning yourself about your vocation, you should concern yourself with getting sin out of your life, or at least you should begin that struggle if you have not already.[33] Again, don't let any particular sin with which you struggle deter you from vocational discernment, but the process can only begin in earnest when you are taking the moral struggle seriously. The fight against sin can be daunting at first, but when you really enter into the interior battle with your sinful passions, it turns into the adventure of a lifetime. Within you there is a whole reality that most people are unaware of until they have begun to really struggle with their sins, and this reality is well worth exploring. The setbacks and victories, the ingenuities and follies, and the perseverance and precariousness of the interior life provide constant material to keep you engaged and fighting.

So what are the best ways to fight against sin in your life?

As St. Augustine says, "Nothing whatever pertaining to godliness and real holiness can be accomplished without grace," and the primary way to receive grace is by partaking of the sacraments. The first and most effective way to get sin out of your life is the frequent reception of the sacrament of Penance. If you commit a mortal sin, you should go to confession as soon as possible, and the wisdom of the saints teaches us that if you are striving for holiness, you should go to confession at least once a month even if you haven't committed a mortal sin.

In confession, we receive three particular helps against the sins we have committed. First, the shame of having to tell someone you committed a sin is a good deterrent from committing the same sin again. Second, the particular grace, called the "sacramental grace," of the sacrament of Penance is the help to fight against the sins we have confessed. And third, we can receive the counsel of the priest as to how to fight against the sins in practical ways. If you are struggling with a certain sin, do not be afraid to ask the priest for advice. He studied in the seminary for at least five years and has been hearing confessions for years most likely. He'd probably be happy to share something of what he's learned!

21

Another great tool in fighting against sin is a daily *examen*. An *examen* is basically an examination of conscience like you would do for confession, except that you look not only at where you sinned but also where you resisted temptation. In the daily *examen*, which is usually done at the end of the day, you think through the day asking yourself where you failed and where you succeeded in doing God's will. You ask God's pardon for the times you failed, and you thank God for the times you responded to the grace he gave you to do his will. You then think about the next day and the ways in which you can overcome temptation and improve in doing God's will tomorrow.

◯ *Do's and Don'ts*

The two most common mistakes that people make when discerning a vocation is that they either try to discern God's will when they aren't really striving for holiness in their state in life, or they think that just because they are struggling with a given sin now, they aren't called to a given vocation.

Do: Strive for Holiness Now

In the words of Saint Mother Teresa, "We must have a real living determination to reach holiness."[34] Right now, God is calling you to be a saint. Doing his will in your state in life now will open your eyes to his will for you in the future. Learning how to discern and respond to the will of God in the normal circumstances of daily life should be considered a training ground for discerning the major decision of a vocation: "He who is faithful in a very little is faithful also in much" (Lk 16:10). These little acts of faithfulness train our soul to recognize God's will for us and train our will to respond promptly to God's will when it presents itself to us. Plus, real holiness is required in every vocation. So until you know which vocation God is calling you to, you might as well start working on that universal call to holiness! Time and energy spent improving yourself, rooting out sin, and growing in virtue is never wasted time.

Don't: Think That Just Because You Are Struggling With a Given Sin That You Aren't Called to a Given Vocation.

"Conversion is a continuing obligation for the whole Church. She is holy but includes sinners in her midst."[35] Each vocation requires continual conversion and a continual striving for holiness. Each vocation also has sinners living out that vocation; in fact, nothing but sinners of varying degrees live out the various vocations, religious and otherwise, for, aside from the Blessed Mother, there is not a single human person who is completely untouched by sin. We are all sinners, and yet God calls us each to our own vocation. God "saved us and called us with a holy calling, not in virtue of our works but in virtue of his own purpose and the grace which he gave us in Christ Jesus" (2 Tm 1:9).

A certain amount of feeling unworthiness before a vocation is appropriate. What man is really ready to love his wife "as Christ loved the church" (Eph 5:25)? What woman is prepared to be "subject to [her] husband . . . as the church is subject to Christ" (Eph 5:22, 24)? What woman is worthy to be a consecrated bride of Christ? What man is worthy to stand in the person of Christ the priest as he offers the eternal sacrifice? None of us are worthy of our vocations or able to live up to our vocation perfectly, and God understands that. We can ask—along with Isaiah who exclaimed, "Woe is me! . . . For I am a man of unclean lips" (Is 6:5)—that God send his angel to purify us as he did that great prophet and to say to us, "Behold, this [burning coal] has touched your lips; your guilt is taken away, and your sin forgiven" (Is 6:7). 23

Forgiveness is real, grace is real, and conversion is real. Beg God's grace to make you more worthy of your calling and take up the practical means to remove every stain of sin from your life. The words of Pope St. John Paul II are a fitting conclusion here:

> If, in spite of your personal effort to follow Christ you are sometimes weak and do not live in conformity to the law of love, to the commandments, do not be discouraged. Christ continues to wait for you. He, Jesus, is the Good Shepherd who searches for the lost sheep and who tenderly bears it on his shoulder (see Lk 15:4–7). Christ is the friend who never lets you down.[36]

✪ *Reflection/Discussion Questions*

- Is there a virtue listed above that you would like to understand better? How do you grow in that virtue? What are some of its connected virtues? What is the opposed vice? What are practical ways you could live that virtue in your circumstances?

- What are some of the most intimidating parts of each of the vocations that God could be asking you to live? Do you trust that God will give you the grace necessary to live whatever vocation he has in store for you?

- What are some areas of your life that could use conversion? Have you spoken to a priest or other mentor about how to grow in those areas?

- Do you regularly make use of the sacrament of Penance (at least once a month)? If so, think about how that sacrament has helped you to be freed from sinful tendencies and to grow in virtue. If you do not currently go to confession with any regularity, begin doing so now. If you are unsure of when or how to go to confession, look up confession times on your parish website and search online for a Catholic guide to confession.

- How can you improve your preparation for and reception of Holy Communion to receive more fully the grace available in the Blessed Sacrament?

CHAPTER 3

PRAYER

○ *Lacey*

"Yeah, I'm really not sure what God is calling me to. I ask him all the time, but he's just not telling me."

"Lacey, you don't go to Mass most Sundays."

"Yeah?"

" . . ."

I had to do everything I could to keep myself from laughing. Lacey, a friend of mine from college who had been fairly active in college campus ministry, stopped by to visit me one day in the seminary. She was in that post-college lull in which she had a job that she kind of liked, had a circle of friends that she kind of liked, but wasn't really fulfilled or happy with any of it. She wanted to move on to the rest of her life but didn't know in what direction to go.

She had received enough formation growing up and in college that she knew that "direction" was her vocation and that living her vocation was going to give her that sense of fulfillment she was looking for, but somewhere in the mix, she missed the memo that she had to be close to God in order to be able to understand his will.

Earlier in the conversation, we had updated each other about our lives, what we enjoyed about our situations, what we disliked, and how we were doing in our faith. Lacey had told me that she still had faith in God and still believed that the Catholic Church was the true Church. She said she prayed most days, but getting to Mass on Sunday was just not her highest priority. She knew what she was doing was wrong, but she just didn't really have the motivation to change.

When she dropped the line about not knowing where God was calling her, I didn't even know where to start. The fact that she was concerned about her vocation and that she was asking God for guidance was great, but so many other things about her life were wrong. Luckily, we were still good enough friends that I could poke fun at her about the absurdity of her situation and open her up to talk more about the topic. We talked about the importance of Sunday Mass, the importance of striving for holiness (her moral life was a bit of a mess as well), the basics of discernment, and the importance of finding other people who could support her and remind her to be diligent about all of these things.

26   She took the advice really well and started going to Mass regularly after her visit. Unfortunately, through a mutual friend, I heard that after three months or so, she stopped going to Sunday Mass. Lacey is still working the same mediocre job, has the same mediocre friends, and is still not making any progress in the discernment of her vocation.

The situation with Lacey—that of a person that basically never went to Sunday Mass but still expressed an interest in discerning her vocation—is obviously extreme. However, it is indicative of how some people approach discernment. Before they start discerning, they have no interest whatsoever in drawing close to God. They realize they need to figure out their vocation. Only at that time do they start praying. They pray only about their vocation, and when they find their vocation, they stop praying. Basically, their relationship with God is a friendship of utility using God to get what they want. When he is no longer useful (in their eyes), they stop talking to him. In human terms, we call this "using someone," and it is both unflattering and insulting. If we wouldn't do something that rude to another human person, why would we do it to God?

➲ What Does "Prayer" Have to Do With Vocational Discernment?

If You Never Talk to God, How Are You Going to Know What He Wants?

Let's start with what Lacey had right: prayer is needed to discern God's will. Lacey knew that, as the Compendium states, "It is through prayer that we can discern 'what is the will of God' (Rom 12:2) and have the 'steadfastness to do it' (Heb 10:36)."[37] Just as we don't know what a person with whom we've never spoken would want, we have no idea what God wants if we don't speak to him. Think of all of the possibilities for miscommunication if you were to go up to a human being you don't know and ask them what they want. What if they don't speak English? What if they are taken aback by such an abrupt question and don't tell you their deepest desires but rather only superficial desires or only a part of what they want? What if by differences in communication styles, they say what they really want, but you don't completely understand what they are saying?

27

There are so many variables in communication among humans that if you really want to understand someone, it's better to make sure you have a good and healthy relationship with them. If that is the case with humans, how much more so with God? Job warns us well, "For God speaks in one way, and in two, though man does not perceive it" (Jb 33:14). God is constantly communicating to us, but we don't always perceive it because the language of God is a particular language. As Blessed John Henry Newman says, God, "both in nature and in grace, speaks to us behind a veil."[38] It is not easy to understand what God desires of us in matters that are not part of the public revelation of Jesus Christ (i.e., Scripture and Tradition). We have to learn the "language" of God in order to discern to which vocation he is calling us, and learning that language takes time.

In order to learn a language well, you have to immerse yourself in it. To learn God's language means immersing yourself in prayer. You don't have to go to a hermitage and cut yourself off completely from the world to learn how to communicate with God, but you do need to set aside specific times dedicated to prayer. What do you do during these times? Pray! Some of the long-proven ways to pray are the Rosary, the Stations of the Cross, or reading and speaking to God about meditations from great saints such as St. Alphonsus Liguori, St. Francis de Sales, St. Augustine of Hippo, or St. Josemaria Escrivá. There have been many other good prayer and meditation books written over the centuries. If you're not sure which one to choose, find a well-formed Catholic whom you trust and ask them for a suggestion.

One form of prayer that is particularly useful when discerning a vocation is *Lectio Divina*. *Lectio Divina* is essentially actively reading the Scriptures and entering into a conversation with God about that piece of Scripture. *Lectio* is often explained as having four steps: 1) Read; 2) Apply; 3) Speak; 4) Listen. The first step is simply to read the passage of Scripture. Take your time reading it. God doesn't rush, and neither should we when we are spending time with him. You can read the passage several times, almost to the point where you have it memorized. The second step is to apply the passage to yourself. This can be done in two ways (both are acceptable!): either by entering into the historical event that the passage is describing or by applying that passage to your own life.

For example, consider the passage in John 8:1–11, in which the scribes and Pharisees bring a woman to Jesus whom they are going to stone for the sin of adultery, and Jesus starts writing in the dust. You could imagine yourself entering into the scene by being one of the people holding the stones, ready to put the woman to death. Jesus begins writing in the sand, and all of the people around you begin to drop their stones and walk away.

What is Jesus writing? Everyone else has left, and you stand there alone. Will you drop your stone?

Or you could think about how to apply that scene to your own life. Others have thrown you down at the feet of Jesus, condemning your sins. What sin are you most ashamed of? What sin do you think nobody would forgive? Do you feel thrown down at the feet of God for condemnation? Jesus does not condemn you. He forgives your sin through the sacrament of Penance. He turns away all of those who want to condemn you. But he does not tell you to go and continue in your sin. He says to you as well, "Go, and do not sin again" (Jn 8:11).

The third step of *Lectio Divina* is to speak to God about the experience of step two, "Apply." Do you struggle with being judgmental? Do you struggle with forgiving others who have offended you? Do you struggle with a certain sin? Do you struggle with forgiving yourself for what you have done in the past or for the sins that you are caught in now? Tell our Lord. He already knows, but he wants you to speak with him about it.

The fourth step of *Lectio Divina* is to listen. Don't expect to hear any noises. God does speak through extraordinary phenomena sometimes, but most of the time he speaks to us through the movements of our soul, specifically the intellect and will. When God uses extraordinary phenomena to communicate his will, it's typically because the person with whom he is trying to communicate is thick headed: he sent the plagues on Pharaoh because he didn't listen the first time; he sent the prophets to Israel because they would not heed his word; and most Eucharistic miracles happen because someone involved doubts the real presence of Christ in the Eucharist. Moral of the story: don't force God to use extraordinary phenomena to communicate with you.[39] Just learn to listen to him in your heart. During this time of listening, certain things may become clear in your mind. You may be moved to make a firm resolution to turn away from a certain sin or do some good work, or you may end up just sitting there receiving God's love. Whatever happens, this step is very important and should not be neglected just because it feels like nothing is happening.

Pray Constantly

In the words of St. Evagrius, "We have not been commanded to work, to keep watch and to fast constantly, but it has been laid down that we are to pray without ceasing."[40] If we consider prayer to be restricted to the recited prayers that we have memorized or a silent period of meditation on some passage of Scripture, the command of 1 Thes 5:17 to "pray constantly" can seem burdensome, and frankly a bit boring. However, prayer should not be restricted to those periods of time that we set aside specifically for prayer.

While some people may be called to a vocation in which prayer is a major part of their schedule, nobody can spend all of their time praying the liturgy, reciting the Rosary, and doing *Lectio Divina*. Even the most contemplative monks and religious are required to spend much of their day working within the confines of their cloister for the upkeep and maintenance of the monastery. Contemplatives have to learn how to pray in the midst of their daily duties, just as a husband and wife need to learn how to pray in the midst of the duties and events of family life. Not only will constant prayer help you to soak yourself in the "language" of God so you can better understand his will, but learning to pray constantly now will also help you to live your vocation well in the future, no matter where God is calling you.

So how does one pray constantly? The most common method is often referred to as "spontaneous prayers." Spontaneous prayers are little prayers that you offer up throughout the day silently or in some cases out loud. As St. Therese of Lisieux writes, "Prayer is a surge of the heart; it is a simple look turned toward heaven, it is a cry of recognition and of love, embracing both trial and joy."[41] Therefore, any spontaneous "surge of the heart," "look turned toward heaven," or "cry of recognition and of love" is a spontaneous prayer. Some of the formulas suggested by the saints to be used as spontaneous prayers are: "Lord, I love you."; "Thank you Lord!"; "God, come to my assistance!"; or "Not my will, but yours be done." Praying these prayers throughout the day—even hundreds of times a day—keeps your mind constantly directed toward God.

But what about the time between the spontaneous prayers? Even if you pray hundreds of spontaneous prayers throughout the day, there will still be moments in which you aren't saying a prayer. The simple fact is, at points in our life, we are required to give 100 percent of our attention to a certain task, or at other moments we simply don't have the ability to direct our hearts actively toward God, such as when we are sleeping. How do we turn those moments into a prayer?

At the beginning of each day, we can make a virtual intention to offer up the entire day to our Lord. A virtual intention is like a background intention. It means that we may not have the intention on our minds at all times, but because we have decided to live our lives in a certain way, that intention takes precedence unless there is an opposing intention in our lives. So, for example, you can have the virtual intention to offer your entire day to our Lord, but when you are laboring over a calculus equation, you are not thinking about offering that moment to our Lord. You are thinking, "Why in the world is calculus so complicated!"

31

In that case, doing calculus is not contrary to offering the day to our Lord, so the virtual intention still applies, and that moment is still offered to our Lord. If, however, you make the virtual intention to offer the day to our Lord, and in a moment of passion decide to stuff yourself with sixteen Oreos, the actual intention of eating sixteen Oreos is gluttonous and contrary to doing the will of God. Therefore, that action of eating sixteen Oreos is not offered up to our Lord.

The traditional way to make that virtual intention at the beginning of the day is to pray the morning offering. A simple children's version of the morning offering is, "Dear Jesus, this day is for you. Help me in everything I think, say, and do." Or a more common morning offering is:

> O my God, through the Immaculate Heart of Mary, I offer you my prayers, works, joys, and sufferings of this day, in union with the Holy Sacrifice of the Mass offered throughout the world. I offer them for the intentions of your Sacred Heart, the salvation of souls, and the reparation of sins. I offer them for all bishops and apostles of prayer and, in particular, for the recommendations made by the Holy Father for this month.

Either version works as long as you truly pray the prayer and make the virtual intention to offer up your entire day to our Lord.

Get to Know God

32

Imagine if a young man in college saw an attractive young lady on the first day of class, walked up to her, and asked, "Am I supposed to marry you?" While the girl may think the absurdity of the question is cute, the absurdity of the question still remains. Nobody seriously asks a person to marry them the first time they talk. Step one is to introduce yourself, have some sort of a conversation, and then, if things go well, get to know each other better. If things go smashingly well, you can eventually break the marriage question, but you don't get to that point until you are fairly well along in the relationship.

It works the same way with God. Get to know God before you start asking vocation questions. If you've never really had a life of prayer before, then it's probably better to hold off on the vocation questions until you get to know God a little more. You get to know God by time spent with him in prayer, or what is commonly called "having a prayer life." What does having a prayer life look like for a single person? Each person's prayer life will look a little bit different based on their particular circumstances. The basic parts of a healthy prayer life are: regular attendance at Mass, frequent confession, some daily recited devotional prayers, a regular period of mental prayer, and constant prayer throughout the day.

The Holy Sacrifice of the Mass is the center of the Christian life and is the source and summit of the Church's prayer. We are all required to attend Mass every Sunday unless we have a serious reason to be excused. Mass is also offered every day in almost every parish throughout the world. It's good to try to make it to daily Mass at least once a week. If you've never been to Mass on a day other than Sunday, try it out! Daily Masses are usually only thirty minutes long, the homily is shorter, but you still are able to be present at the Holy Sacrifice and to receive Communion. Some people may not be able to make it to a Mass during the week because of work or other restrictions, while others may be able to make it to make it to Mass every day of the week. The point is not how often you are able to make it but rather that you are being generous to our Lord with your time and that you are regularly attending Mass and receiving our Lord in Communion.

Along with Communion, the sacrament that a Catholic most frequently receives today is the sacrament of Penance. The sacrament of Penance is such a powerful source of grace, and it is the means our Lord gives us to access the forgiveness he won for us on the cross. God wants us to receive the forgiveness of our sins through the sacrament of Penance. Just as with a human being whom you have seriously offended, the only way to repair that relationship is to humbly go to them and ask for their forgiveness, so also with God. Whenever you have seriously offended him by a mortal sin, the only way to repair that relationship is to go humbly to him and ask for his forgiveness in the sacrament of Penance.

However, you shouldn't only go to confession when you commit mortal sins; the wisdom of the saints teaches us that you should go to confession at least once a month. Just as someone in a healthy relationship frequently asks for forgiveness for the little things they have done to offend the other person, so we should ask God for forgiveness for the little sins in our life on a regular basis. When we confess our venial sins and receive the forgiveness of God in the sacrament of Penance, we are freed from those sins, and we receive a particular grace that helps us not to commit those sins again. It may take time, and "old habits die hard" as the saying goes, but you will be amazed at the miracles God can work in you if you cooperate with the grace he gives through the sacraments!

The written prayers that have been passed down through the Church over the centuries are some of the greatest treasures of Christian devotion. Devotional prayers such as the Our Father, Hail Mary, Glory Be, Morning Offering, St. Michael Prayer, Prayer to Your Guardian Angel, the Angelus, and countless other prayers not only are outstanding ways to pray but also form our desires and teach us how to pray in our own words. Any good Catholic prayer book will have many written devotional prayers. Memorize a handful of these prayers and recite them daily as part of your prayer life. If you get tired of them or you find that the prayers are becoming stale and dry from repetition, you can memorize different prayers and recite those instead. The important thing is that you are praying and being formed by the prayer tradition of the Church.

A specific period of time set apart for mental prayer is also an indispensable part of the prayer life of anyone discerning their vocation. The Rosary, and the accompanying meditations on the mysteries of the life of Christ, is one of the most renowned forms of mental prayer. The Stations of the Cross are another great form of mental prayer, particularly fitting for Fridays and the season of Lent. *Lectio Divina*, in which one meditates on a passage of the Scriptures using the four steps—1) read, 2) apply, 3) speak, 4) listen—is yet another. And lastly, any good book of meditations written by a saint or trusted spiritual author can provide much material for mental prayer.

A good minimum to aim for is one hour or more of mental prayer per week. That could be a weekly holy hour spent in front of the Blessed Sacrament praying the Rosary, reading a book of meditations and doing *Lectio Divina*. It could simply be a couple of Rosaries a week and a thirty-minute period of *Lectio Divina*. Or it could be a couple of Rosaries, a period of reading a book of meditations, and a period of *Lectio Divina*. Because it takes time for the soul to settle down and really immerse itself in the presence of God, it's better to not break up the periods of mental prayer into anything shorter than fifteen minutes. If you find yourself desiring or practicing more mental prayer than an hour a week, great! Each person will have a different propensity and availability for mental prayer based on different personality traits and circumstances, but one hour a week is a good minimum to aim for.

Lastly, every Christian should strive to offer every moment of their day to our Lord. Spontaneous prayers offered throughout the day and the frequent renewal of the virtual intention to offer the entire day up to our Lord are the most common ways to pray constantly. The morning offering recited as one of the memorized devotional prayers is a good way to make and renew that virtual intention.

The spiritual life is not a cookie cutter formula. The spiritual and devotional lives of different individuals will look, well, different, and each person's spiritual life will likely change as the circumstances of their life change. The basic building blocks outlined above are the essentials and some of the most important parts of a healthy spiritual life. Maintaining these practices over a period of time will help to develop and maintain a relationship with God while forming the right context in which you can begin to ask God about your vocation.

◐ *Do's and Don'ts*

The two most common mistakes that people make when discerning a vocation is that they try to figure out where God is calling them without having any real prayer life, and if they do have a prayer life, they *only* ask God about their vocation.

Do: Develop a Life of Prayer for Its Own Sake

St. Augustine teaches us that "God wills that our desire should be exercised in prayer, that we may be able to receive what he is prepared to give."[42] Before we are able to understand the will of God, we need to be "exercised in prayer." Prayer life comes first; vocational discernment follows.

Having a prayer life is not just a means to the end of "finding" your vocation. That would be using your relationship with God to get what you want. God would become a mere tool that you use to get something else, which is utterly contrary to his dignity. God isn't a means, he's an end. The purpose of developing a prayer life is to grow closer to God. Period. Not to get to what we really want out of him. It does just so happen that you must have a real relationship with him in order to understand his will, but that is not why you should develop that relationship with him.

If you just developed a life of prayer to get from God the knowledge of your vocation, you would quickly become frustrated that he has not immediately revealed it to you. Evagrius Ponticus responds, "Do not be troubled if you do not immediately receive from God what you ask him; for he desires to do something even greater for you, while you cling to him in prayer."[43] The greater thing that God desires for us is the relationship itself: the life of grace and love that opens up in our lives when we are truly in love with a God who has given us everything out of love and who continues to pour forth his spiritual and temporal blessings upon us. The relationship has to remain primary, and the discernment has to be secondary. In the words of St. John Paul II:

Look for him in prayer, in sincere and assiduous dialogue with him. Let him share in the questions that come up, your problems, and your own plans. Look for him in his word, in the Gospels, and in the liturgical life of the Church. Have recourse to the sacraments. Confidently open your most intimate aspirations to the Love of Christ who waits for you in the Eucharist. You will receive the answer to all your worries and you will see with joy that the consistency of your life which he asks of you is the door to fulfill the noblest dreams of your youth.[44]

Don't: Pray Only About Your Vocation

God doesn't like telemarketing either. Just as a relationship with God shouldn't be developed only for the sake of knowing his will, so also, when praying, we shouldn't spend all of our time asking him what our vocation is. Imagine if you had a boyfriend or girlfriend who only wanted to talk to you about getting married. You tried to change the subject, but they just wanted to know when, where, how, and they wanted absolute certainty. That boyfriend or girlfriend would quickly become irritating, and your relationship would come to a standstill because the other person refused to allow any further depth to develop in the relationship. While getting married is an important topic to bring up if two people are in a serious relationship, it certainly should not be the only thing they talk about! In our relationship with God, it works the same way. If we are constantly asking him about our vocation—who we are supposed to marry, what religious order we should enter, or whether we should enter the diocesan seminary—it stalls both our relationship with God and the discernment process.

Typically, people who spend a lot of time praying about their vocation are also stressing out about their vocation. While you may like to know now what God created you to be, if you are praying and striving to live his will in the daily circumstances of your life, and he hasn't communicated that to you, then he doesn't want you to know right now. It's a painful spot to be in, but it is a spot in which we learn to trust our Lord. The Scriptures tell us to trust again and again, to simply . . .

> Trust in [the Lord], and he will act. (Ps 37:5)

> And if we know that he hears us in whatever we ask, we know that we have obtained the requests made of him. (1 Jn 5:15)

> Therefore I tell you, whatever you ask in prayer, believe that you receive it, and you will. (Mk 11:24)

> Have no anxiety about anything, but in everything by prayer and supplication with thanksgiving let your requests be made known to God. And the peace of God, which passes all understanding, will keep your hearts and your minds in Christ Jesus. (Phil 4:6–7)

If you are struggling in this period of unknowing, know that it will not last forever, and thank God for the opportunity to grow in trust of him.

As a rule of thumb, you are definitely spending too much time worrying about your vocation if you spend more than 50 percent of time in prayer praying about it. A much healthier percentage would be closer to 25 percent for someone who is in a place to act on a certain vocation, and for someone who cannot enter any vocation in the near future (i.e., if you have not reached the last years of high school or have other practical barriers to entering any vocation), a healthy percentage would be less than 10 percent of your total prayer time. God speaks first through the reality of the world around us: if you can't act right now, he doesn't want you to act right now, and you shouldn't worry yourself too much about the distant future because "tomorrow will be anxious for itself. Let the day's own trouble be sufficient for the day." (Mt 6:34).

✪ Reflection/Discussion Questions

- Do you ask God about your vocation?

- Are you convinced that the vocation to which God is calling you will bring you the greatest happiness and fulfillment in life?

- What does your prayer look like now? How could you improve your prayer life? What are the concrete details that an improved prayer life would have?

- How often do you attend Mass? Is there a Mass during the week that you could attend?

- How often do you go to confession? When and where are confessions offered in your area?

- Do you regularly make your morning offering? Which version of the morning offering do you know?

- What are some of your favorite or most common spontaneous prayers?

- Have you tried praying with the method called *Lectio Divina*? How did it go? Have you sought guidance on how to use that form of meditating on the Scriptures more effectively?

CHAPTER 4

TIME

○ *John*

John was an "over-discerner" to say the least. He had grown up in a Catholic family and was well aware of the importance of vocational discernment. The problem was that he wanted to know exactly where God was calling him immediately so that he could begin living his vocation right then.

I met John while he was studying at a good Catholic college. He was beginning his sophomore year. After the normal pleasantries, he immediately started asking me for advice on discernment. Was he called to married life or celibacy? How would he know if he met the right girl? Which order is right for him? Is he called to the priesthood? He had read every book on discernment he could get his hands on and, in general, had a good understanding of how to discern a vocation. The problem was he wanted to know now, not when God wanted him to know.

We kept in touch, and over the next few years he would occasionally call me in a panic. One time, he had met a girl and, after talking to her once, wanted to know if he was meant to marry her. Another time, he had met a priest that really inspired him, and he wanted to know if he should leave college in the middle of the semester to enter the seminary. And a third time, he had finished reading the biography of Saint Francis and called asking which Franciscan order he should join. A few times he called simply because he was fed up with all of the confusion revolving around God's call. Each time he called, I would talk him off of the "vocational ledge" and get him to think a little more clearly: the step after meeting a girl is not to ask about marriage but to get to know her better; seminary runs on an academic schedule, so it's better to wait until closer to the end of the academic year, and if you still are interested in joining the seminary, you can apply to a diocese; before applying to join a religious order, it's best to make a few visits to get to know that particular community.

John truly cared about making the right vocational choice, which is the right disposition to have; the problem was that he was not willing to trust that God would bring him to his vocation at the proper time. John wanted to know what he was supposed to do, and he wanted to know now.

Over the years, John calmed down a little bit and did learn to trust that God would work in his own time. On a "European adventure" trip that John made with a friend of his during the summer after his junior year, he happened to visit the Institute of Christ the King (mostly so that he could have a solid roof over his head and a few warm meals!). He fell in love with the charism of the Institute and their community life. Throughout his senior year, he visited the community a few more times. He made an extended visit after his senior year and now is in formation for the Institute and doing quite well.

God always had a plan for John. He just didn't want him to act until the time was right. That time of waiting was instrumental in helping John to grow in trust, and the foundation in humanities that John received during his college years will help him to be a great religious and a great priest.

◌ *What Does Time Have to Do With Vocational Discernment?*

For Humans, Things Just Take Time

Think about how long it takes a child to learn how to read. A very intelligent child can begin to understand the letters on a page within the course of a year, but he or she is still at a very basic reading level. Humans spend much of their time in school and even through college learning how to read at increasingly higher levels—learning how to interpret words and truly understand what the author is communicating. If it takes that long to learn how to understand the plainly written words of a human author, how much more so should it take time to understand the Divine Author's movements of grace in your intellect and will? Learning to discern takes time.

So, what to do? Just how do you learn to understand the movements of grace in your intellect and will? The same way you learn to read or, truth be told, learn to do anything new: 1) by setting aside dedicated time for that purpose and 2) by turning to great teachers.

There are certain moments in a person's life in which God tends to communicate his will most clearly—namely, when you can actually act on God's call at that moment or in the near future. (I wrote *tends*. It does not always happen that way.) For example, many young men feel called to enter the seminary during their last year or so of high school, and many young couples receive the clarity necessary to begin engagement as they are finishing college. During that time when you are approaching a point in your life that you can act on a call, it is good to set aside dedicated time to discern a particular vocation. Just as when your mind was developed enough to begin to read, your parents sent you to school to have dedicated time to learn, so also when your life has developed to the point where you are ready to make a vocational choice, you have to set aside time to "learn" your vocation.

43

If you already have a relationship with our Lord and a sufficiently developed prayer life, six months to a year is a good amount of time for this dedicated time of discernment. This dedicated time is set aside to ask our Lord to make a tendency toward a particular vocation into a concrete call. If you have felt attracted to religious life, then during that time ask our Lord, "Which religious order are you calling me to?" If you have been developing a relationship with a girl or guy, you could set that time aside to ask our Lord, "Are you calling me to marry this girl or guy? And are you calling her or him to marry me?" (He or she would obviously need to be asking our Lord the same questions about you!) Focus on one particular vocation: priesthood in a particular diocese, entering a particular religious order, marrying a particular person. If you get a really clear answer before the end of the dedicated period, thanks be to God! If you get no answer by the end of the dedicated period, then your answer is "not right now" and thanks be to God! You can continue with the regular course of events, such as going to whichever college fits you best, getting a job, or continuing in your job.

Although the dedicated time for discernment is important, we don't only discern during that time. Just as a functioning human being reads outside of school (at least signs and other things of the sort), so also a functioning Christian should be open to God's calling outside of a dedicated time of discernment. Unless a person is already in their vocation, they should always be open to wherever God is calling them. From the day of your birth until the day of your marriage, final profession, or ordination, God could call you in a different direction. Think of Abraham who, in fulfilling God's will, gathered the wood, climbed the mountain, built the altar, and just as he was raising his hand to sacrifice his son, God called him to stop (see Gn 22:1–19). What a mess it would have been if Abraham had refused to listen to God's will at that time!

Also, just as we needed teachers when learning to read, so also we need teachers to help us read the movements of grace in

44

our souls. A priest, religious, or any well-formed Catholic[45] that you can trust and talk to on occasion is indispensable to help you in the particulars of your vocational discernment. Just as a good teacher wouldn't read for the child, this person can't tell you exactly what your vocation is, but he or she can help you to understand what is happening in your soul so that you can read the movements of God's grace within you.

Even with a great teacher sitting at your side, it will be important to know some of the theory of how to discern. St. Ignatius of Loyola's *Spiritual Exercises* is a magnum opus on discernment. Ignatius talks about three "times" of discernment, but they are better understood as three "ways" that God speaks to a person. They can be described as: 1) a supernatural phenomenon that directs a person to a particular vocation; 2) discernment of the movements of the Holy Spirit in the will; 3) a prudent choice of a vocation as a means of serving God and saving one's soul.[46]

The first two work first in our will and then in our intellect. The third works in our intellect first and then in our will.[47] An example of the first "time" of discernment could be if someone hears a voice, has a vision, or walks away from a period of prayer with an unforgettable conviction that they are called to a certain vocation.[48] This first way is the least certain because the devil and the human psyche can cause things of this sort and, therefore, lead the soul astray. It is very difficult to discern the origin of these types of phenomena, and therefore it's better not to rely on them for guidance.[49]

The second "time" is connected to what is commonly called "discernment." In those intimate moments with God after going to confession or receiving Communion, ask God where he is calling you. When all you want to do is fulfill God's will, where do you feel most attracted? This "time," or way, is more secure than the first, but we can still be misled by our will, which is fickle at times and does not always choose what is best. The third "time" is when we use our reason to look at the different vocations, our own circumstances, and the possibilities available

45

to us in choosing the vocation that seems most in accord with God's will. For example, a man who, despite having a healthy love and respect for the celibate vocations, feels no attraction to them. He finishes college and looks at his circumstances and says to himself: "I have been dating Cathy for the last year. She is a good Catholic woman. She helps me grow in holiness. She loves me, and I love her. The job offer I just received would bring in enough income to support a family. There are no other reasons that I should not propose to her. Therefore, I think God's will for me is to take the next step toward marriage with this woman and propose to her." This third way is the most secure way, assuming we give the benefit of the doubt toward the objectively better or higher vocations.[50] Even if God seems to reveal his will to the soul in one of the first two ways, the third way should be used to confirm God's call.[51]

Timing Is Everything

"In comedy, as in life, timing is everything."[52] The proper use of a pregnant pause, the right rhythm for the punch line, or the pace of one's speech can be the elements that make or break a joke. Sometimes timing can even change the meaning of a joke. While we all hope that our lives aren't a joke, we all appreciate a good laugh. And I think it's reasonable to say that God feels the same way. Why else would platypuses exist?

If timing is important in comedy, how much more so should it be important in vocational discernment? Circumstances are constantly changing, and God in his providence is constantly moving people through his grace to carry forward the history of salvation. An anticipated or delayed response would offset the process and cause unnecessary confusion and heartache. While God is able to work with our always less-than-perfect response to his love, it is always best to respond to his will as promptly as is reasonably possible.

Think of St. Joseph, who, immediately after being instructed by the angel, took Mary and Jesus to Egypt to protect them from Herod (see Mt 2:13–18). Had Joseph not acted in time, God certainly would have found a way to protect our Lord and the Blessed Mother from Herod's guards, but think of all of the difficulty that could have resulted if Joseph had not taken them away quickly enough? Or consider the Blessed Mother, who "went with haste into the hill country" to visit Elizabeth. Had she not arrived to Elizabeth while Elizabeth was still pregnant, we would not have received Mary's beautiful hymn of the Magnificat that Luke records. On the other hand, think of Abram and Sarah, who knew that God would make of Abram a great nation but were not willing to wait until God's time. Sarah gave Abram her slave, Hagar, to bear him children. This attempt to do the will of God on her own time caused Sarah much grief. Hagar "looked with contempt on [Sarah]," and Sarah was so upset that she sent off Hagar and her son Ishmael into the wilderness (Gn 21:14). All of this could have been avoided if Sarah and Abram simply had trusted in God and done things according to his time.

It works similarly in our own vocations. Think back to chapter 1 of this book. God has a plan for you, and it is far better than your own plan. God knows all of the unforeseen consequences, circumstances, and details of your life. He will give you clarity in your vocation in time for you to do his will at the right time. To respond to his will right when he asks is the best thing for you and for everyone around you. However, doing someone else's will is not always easy. In order to be able to respond promptly and fully to God's will, we need what St. Francis de Sales calls "resignation" or its perfection: "holy indifference."[53]

Resignation to the will of God is an act of faith in which we say, "God, I don't understand why, but I trust in your loving providence." It is the virtue that helps us to trust God's plan more than our own and to desire his will more than our own. Holy indifference is the perfection of resignation. Holy indifference is not only to love God's will above your own will but to love only God's will.[54] Pray to grow in the virtue of resignation

47

and hope to achieve holy indifference. Pray for it! Pray about it! Practice it! As with all virtues, the first and most important way to grow in resignation to God's will is to ask him for the grace of resignation. In prayer, we can also exercise the virtue of resignation by making acts of the will that align our will with that of God. We can say to him, "Lord, not my will, but yours be done!", "Lord, show me your will and give me the grace to do it!", or "Lord, I love your will!"

We can practice resignation first by not always choosing our own will. When going out with friends, don't choose the restaurant. When asked to do something you don't want to, simply do it (assuming it's not sinful). When things don't go your way, accept them and move on without complaining. Another way to practice resignation is to think about evil in the world and understand it within God's providence. In the world there is war, death, hunger, suffering, sadness, and difficulty, yet we know that we have an all-loving and all-powerful God that directs all things to the greater good. When you hear about these evil things in the world, try to understand ways that God might be working the greater good through them. If you can't think of any way that good could come from the situation, make an act of trust in God's loving providence. Say to him, "Lord, I don't understand what you are doing here, but I trust you." The virtue of resignation slowly grows in our hearts through prayer and practice, and it prepares us to respond promptly to God's will regarding our vocation when he reveals it to us.

God Works On His Own Time

"Patience is the companion of wisdom" according to St. Augustine, and to discern well, you need a lot of both. God has a plan for you and for every creature, but he doesn't necessarily reveal the details of that plan to you when you would like. In these moments of waiting, you simply need to fortify your faith that God has a particular plan for you, that he loves you more than you love yourself, and that he will reveal his plan to you when it is time as long as you are listening. Then be patient!

As the Catechism says, "Time is in the Father's hands" (CCC 2659). From the beginning of time and throughout all of history, God has had a plan. Creation was intentionally structured to support humanity (see Gn 1–2). Immediately after Adam and Eve sinned and went against God's plan, God promised a new plan—a savior that would crush the head of the serpent (see Gn 3:15). God had a plan for Abraham and his descendants (see Gn 17). God had a plan for David and his kingdom (see 2 Sm 7:8ff). God had a plan for your salvation and the salvation of all men:

> But when the time had fully come, God sent forth his Son, born of woman, born under the law, to redeem those who were under the law, so that we might re- ceive adoption as sons. . . . So through God you are no longer a slave but a son, and if a son then an heir. (Gal 4:4–5, 7)

49

You are an heir of God's promises and plans. If God has had a plan through all of these millennia, and he has made you an heir of all of these plans, why would he not have a particular plan for your life? "Are not two sparrows sold for a penny? And not one of them will fall to the ground without your Father's will. . . . Fear not, therefore; you are of more value than many sparrows" (Mt 10:29–30) and, "You were ransomed . . . not with perishable things such as silver or gold, but with the precious blood of Christ" (1 Pt 1:18–19). If you are really that precious to our Lord, you can bet that he has a plan for your life and that it will be well worth the wait.

Why does God take so long sometimes? I'm not sure. Ask him. What is certain is that he is taking his time for a reason, and that is the best thing for you and for everyone else. Perhaps God is waiting for the proper circumstances to align for you to truly fall in love with your vocation. Perhaps God is allowing your future spouse to grow in the virtues necessary to be a good husband or wife. Perhaps he is waiting for you to grow in the patience, wisdom, and trust required for you to live your vocation well. When Jesus raised Lazarus from the dead, he waited four days beyond when Martha and Mary asked him to come save their brother. Nobody else knew why Jesus would wait so long to come save his friend, but he knew, "This illness is not unto death; it is for the glory of God, so that the Son of God may be glorified by means of it." Pope St. John Paul II points out another possibility:

> It is easy to be consistent for a day or two. It is difficult and important to be consistent for one's whole life. It is easy to be consistent in the hour of enthusiasm; it is difficult to be so in the hour of tribulation. And only a consistency that lasts . . . can be called faithfulness.[55]

50

That consistency may be what God is teaching you now so that you can be consistent in your vocation. Every vocation requires patience, consistency, and a dogged perseverance to live it faithfully. We can be certain that God knows what he's doing, and we just need to trust him. In the words of St. Francis de Sales, "If we always try to keep our will very firm in wanting to discover the good that has been shown to us, God will not fail to make all redound to his glory."[56]

◔ *Do's and Don'ts*

It is key to set aside a dedicated period of time to discern a particular vocation when the opportunity to follow what was previously only an inclination is approaching. However, it is also key to recognize and accept that God might not give a clear answer during that period.

Do: Set Aside a Period of Time to
Discern a Particular Vocation

If you are in a situation or approaching a situation in which you could take concrete steps to enter a vocation (such as getting engaged, entering the seminary, or requesting to enter a religious order), and you have a tendency toward one or a small number of possible vocations, set aside time to discern the right path. St. Ignatius of Loyola wrote the *Spiritual Exercises* as a thirty-day silent retreat made for the purpose of discerning one's vocation. Today, few people have the self-control to be quiet for that long or the freedom to step away from the world for a period of thirty days. However, most people can set aside a period of six months to a year in which they pray and discern in a more dedicated way about a particular vocation while living their normal life.

The dedicated time should start with a clear yes or no question to God. For example, "Do you want me to petition to join religious order X now?" "Do you want me to propose to Mary now?" "Do you want me to enter the seminary for this diocese now?" In certain circumstances, it might be OK to list a few different but similar options (in particular when it comes to religious orders or dioceses—good luck finding a girl that is OK with you dating multiple ladies at the same time!): "Do you want me to join religious order X, Y, or Z?" "Do you want me to join the seminary for the Diocese of X or Z?" Guidelines for how to discern during this period are given in this chapter and in the following chapters. By following these guidelines, over time your desire for the particular vocation that you are discerning will likely increase or decrease, your motives for choosing or rejecting that particular vocation will become purer, and you will likely come to a reasonable certainty about whether God is calling you to that vocation.

51

Don't: Think That God Has to Answer Your Prayers During That Period of Time

That reasonable certainty that gives us enough confidence to act on a particular vocation is not something that we can force. God works on his own time. By setting a fixed time, you are not saying to God, "You better tell me the plan by that date, or else!" You are setting aside a particular period of time to listen more attentively to his call. At the end of that dedicated period of time, things might be super clear, and they might not be clear! You might still have no idea where God is calling you. You might still have all of the same questions and doubts that you had before. If that is the case, then it is not that God is not listening to you or that you did something wrong. Sometimes God just wants us to continue down the normal path of our lives, and in that case, he doesn't tell us anything. Yes, that can be a little bit annoying, but at moments like that we simply have to fortify our trust in God, recognize that he has a plan for us (even if he's not telling it to us now), and continue to be open to his will.

52

✪ Reflection/Discussion Questions

- Do you regularly speak with someone about your vocation? If not, who are some people that you could speak to about the topic? If so, are they the right people?

- What are some good books on discernment? If you don't know any, ask a priest, religious, or well-formed Catholic for some suggestions.

- Is there a particular vocation that you feel a tendency toward? What is it?

- Are you in a situation where you could take concrete steps to enter a vocation?

- What are some things that that you could do to clarify your vocation?

- Have you ever visited a religious house or seminary for a discernment retreat?

- In prayer and when you are closest to God, what vocation is most attractive to you?

CHAPTER 5

TALK

◔ *Samantha*

Samantha finished college a year ago and was not quite sure where God was calling her. While in college she developed a good friendship with one of the sisters in a nearby convent. Samantha wanted to dedicate herself to Christ in some way, but she really wasn't sure how she was meant to do so.

Despite several people suggesting to her that she get a spiritual director, or at least regularly speak to someone about her vocation, she refused. She had never had a spiritual director. Her parents were good Catholics, and they never had a spiritual director. She knew lots of good Catholics from her home town, and they didn't have a spiritual director. Why should she have one? Plus, the whole experience of having to tell someone about what was going on inside of her just sounded unpleasant. She would much rather just figure things out on her own.

While I was not her spiritual director, I was her friend, and one day I got her to open up a little bit about her vocation:

"I think I might be called to religious life."

"Yeah, which community?"

"Well, the red sisters would make the most sense, but I don't really want to join them." That's what we called the community she was friendly with.

"Why not?"

"I'm not sure . . ."

"Samantha, you've been thinking about this for a year and still don't know why you don't want to join them?"

"To tell you the truth, I don't want to join because their habit is ugly!" She blurted out. We stared at each other for a moment and then just burst out laughing. Admittedly, their habit was pretty ugly. . . .

We kept talking, and she revealed that she actually had never really been able to admit to herself that was the reason she didn't want to join, but after having said it out loud she saw how fickle and vain the reason was. She couldn't come up with any other reasons for not joining the order, and having voiced the concern about the habit, it wasn't as big of a deal to her any more. She lined up a "come and see" retreat to get to know the order better, and within a few months, she was certain she was not called to that order. It turns out she wasn't called to the order, because as she learned more about the charism and the community life of the order, it became less and less attractive to her. She has since made visits to several other religious orders and has narrowed it down to two. Hopefully she will be petitioning to enter one of the two within the next year! And, best of all, now she has a spiritual director.

For Samantha, simply having a frank conversation about her motives for not joining a particular order enabled her to clarify things enough to get that order off of the list of possible vocations and move forward with the discernment process. The conversation only took fifteen minutes, but it was enough to shake her out of the vocational deadlock she had been in for the last year.

○ What Does Talking Have to Do With Vocational Discernment?

Saint Philip Neri once said, "Those who have themselves for a spiritual director have a fool for a spiritual director." Fairly strong words for a saint! After the obvious topics such as fighting against sin, growing in virtue, and prayer, the Scriptures speak most strongly about the importance of talking to some sort of advisor. The following are just some of the examples from Proverbs:

> Fools despise wisdom and instruction. (Prv 1:7)

> Where there is no guidance, a people falls;
>> but in an abundance of counselors there is safety. (Prv 11:14)

> The way of a fool is right in his own eyes,
>> but a wise man listens to advice. (Prv 12:15)

> By insolence the heedless make strife,
>> but with those who take advice is wisdom. (Prv 13:10)

> Without counsel plans go wrong,
>> but with many advisers they succeed. (Prv 15:22)

> Listen to advice and accept instruction,
>> that you may gain wisdom for the future. (Prv 19:20)

57

If having an advisor is so important in general, why would we not seek advice when it comes to the most important decision of our life? We need great wisdom in the moment of choosing our vocation, and as the Scriptures say, "With those who take advice is wisdom" (Prv 13:10). However, speaking to someone about the movements of grace in your soul can seem like a strange practice that nobody else does, or simply a little too revealing for your comfort zone.

From the earliest times of the Church, people would turn to bishops, priests, and holy people for advice on a whole variety of topics. We still have many of the letters of St. Augustine, St. Jerome, and other Fathers of the Church giving guidance and spiritual direction to various virgins, widows, and other Christians.[57] So why is it that so few people have a spiritual director today? One reason is simply the current shortage of priests in first world countries. People recognize that priests are busy and don't want to bother them with the details of their lives. Unfortunately, this "politeness" is only piling up work on priests and religious. Many young people perhaps have felt a call to religious life or priesthood and by not speaking to a priest or religious about the call have been misled and not entered their vocation. This only contributes to the priest and religious shortage. The most "polite" thing you can do for a priest or religious, if you are truly desiring to do God's will and are unsure of where God is calling you, is to actually talk to a priest or religious about your discernment. Don't take up more time than is necessary, but speak to them and ask for their advice, guidance, and prayers.

58
The Desert Fathers wrote profusely on the importance of revealing everything to the "elders" of the community and gave numerous examples of the downfall of monks who chose to keep their experiences to themselves instead of humbly opening themselves up to the advice and guidance of others. One of the more striking stories told by St. John Cassian is that of the old man Heron who was convinced that God was calling him to strict fasting and through that strict fasting exhausted himself to the point that he fell into a well![58] Another example given is that of the unnamed man who had visions of a so called "angel" that deceived the man to the point of almost murdering his own son. Luckily the son caught on to what was happening and fled just in time.[59] Both of these were very holy men, respected by the community, and held in high regard by everyone, but their pride blinded them, and they were not willing to talk to someone about discernment of their interior life.

Navel Gazing Isn't Healthy; It Hurts Your Neck and Gets Lint in Your Eyes

Just as trying to look into your own belly button is a dangerous and futile process, so also is trying to peer into the depths of your soul by yourself. The human soul is so complex that oftentimes when we try to understand what is happening within us, we get lost in a web of fears, desires, emotions, hopes, and pressures. We often end up misleading ourselves. We need a mirror to help us see plainly. That mirror is some person that you can trust and talk to on a somewhat regular basis.

The calling of Samuel is a great example of how this relationship with your spiritual director should go:

> Now the boy Samuel was ministering to the LORD under Eli. . . . And Samuel was lying down within the temple of the LORD, where the ark of God was. Then the LORD called, "Samuel! Samuel!" and he said, "Here I am!" and ran to Eli, and said, "Here I am, for you called me." But he said, "I did not call; lie down again." So he went and lay down. And the LORD called again, "Samuel!" And Samuel arose and went to Eli, and said, "Here I am, for you called me." But he said, "I did not call, my son; lie down again." Now Samuel did not yet know the LORD, and the word of the LORD had not yet been revealed to him. And the LORD called Samuel again the third time. And he arose and went to Eli, and said, "Here I am, for you called me." Then Eli perceived that the LORD was calling the boy. Therefore Eli said to Samuel, "Go, lie down; and if he calls you, you shall say, 'Speak, LORD, for your servant hears.'" So Samuel went and lay down in his place. And the LORD came and stood forth, calling as at other times, "Samuel! Samuel!" And Samuel said, "Speak, for your servant hears." (1 Sm 3:1–10)

59

The first thing to point out is that Samuel had already known Eli for a while. Eli knew Samuel's personality, and Samuel trusted Eli. Next, both Samuel and Eli were "ministering to the Lord." Both of them were serving God and doing his will. Third, it is very interesting that Samuel heard the voice of God, while Eli did not. Only Samuel heard the voice because God was calling him, not Eli. However, Samuel went straight to Eli to talk to him about what he had heard. The next important point is that Samuel got it wrong: he thought that Eli was calling him. Samuel was not able to interpret perfectly the call that he had received. Fifth, Samuel didn't just talk to Eli once, and when Eli didn't make it all clear, run off to talk to someone else. Samuel kept going back to Eli. Over time, Eli was able to understand better what Samuel was experiencing, and helped to guide him to understand that this calling was the calling of the Lord. Lastly, Eli didn't tell Samuel, "God is calling you to be a prophet and the last of the Judges of Israel, you will anoint Saul as king of Israel, then he'll mess things up, so you'll anoint David king. Saul will try to kill David, then he'll conjure you up from the dead. David will get away. Then Saul will die, and David will be king. You're going to have a great life!" He simply directed Samuel to understand better the voice of the Lord: "Go, lie down; and if he calls you, you shall say, 'Speak, LORD, for your servant hears.'"

In the same way, you should know the person with whom you are speaking, and they should know you. It may be that you don't know anyone who could be a good person to talk to, and therefore you may need to introduce yourself to a priest, religious, or other well-formed Catholic to develop a relationship with them and allow them to get to know you.

Next, both you and the person that you speak with about your vocation should be striving to do the will of God. If that piece is not there, then there is no point in discerning. As mentioned in chapter 2, if you disregard God's will in most things, why would he bother communicating his will to you in regard to your vocation?

Third, you can't hope for the other person to tell you exactly what God wants. They are there to help you read the movements of God in your soul. Even though your mentor helps you in the path of discernment, sometimes you might not get it right. They will be there to correct you and help you to understand clearly what is the voice of God and what is not.

Fourth, discernment is not a short process. You will have to go back to talk to the same person multiple times. The persistence of a call is one of the sure signs of a true vocation, and persistence can only be measured over time.

Lastly, if the person that you are speaking with tries to push you in a direction that the evidence you have shown to him or her does not support, beware. On very rare occasions the director will have some sort of supernatural guidance that reveals their directee's vocation to them, but that is very rare. For the most part, they should just help you interpret God's movements in your life. The more normal path of direction is that the director serves as a sounding board, a third party that can see things objectively, and a source of wisdom.

61

Talking Forces You to Think . . . Hopefully!

"Think before you speak" is a maxim that most functioning adults try to live by, and most people do so even more when they are about to reveal something personal about themselves to another person. When we speak to someone else about our desires and thoughts concerning our vocation, we have to grasp what is happening within us before we verbalize it. That said, if you prayerfully prepare for such a talk, often the simple act of talking bears more than half the fruit. Very likely you have experienced that sometimes just "getting something off your chest" or talking it through with a friend clarifies things. As long as you say what you are experiencing in a somewhat coherent way, then already you are doing the most important part of spiritual direction.

This doesn't mean that all of the other characteristics of a good spiritual director can be ignored. As has been mentioned earlier, they should first and foremost desire to do God's will and desire for you to do God's will. They should also have a good Catholic formation. They don't have to be a priest or religious, but they should know well what the Church teaches and have a decent understanding of how human beings work.

It is also very helpful if they know you and your personality. They should know not only how human beings in general work but also how you in particular work: Do you often over-react to or over-state things? Do you say everything all at once, or does it take you time to get everything out? Do you tend to work more on emotions or on reason? What are your strengths? What are your weaknesses? Knowing these sorts of things is essential so your spiritual director can give you good advice.

This may go without saying, but your director should also be wise. It will be normal for a spiritual director to give you advice. It is very beneficial if that director is a wise person. How do you know? Well, one warning sign is that if that person's personal life seems to be something of a mess, that is a good sign that they may not themselves be wise. Or if they "bounced around" a lot in life from vocation to vocation, that may be another warning sign. Or look at other people for whom such a person may have acted as a mentor. How did they turn out? It is not always easy to identify wisdom in a person, but you must try.

And lastly, it is beneficial if they are holy: "Blessed is the man who walks not in the counsel of the wicked, / nor stands in the way of sinners, nor sits in the seat of scoffers" (Ps 1:1). Finding a person who is striving for holiness, is well formed, knows you, is wise, and holy is quite a feat in most communities. The two most important characteristics are that they are wise and holy (or what St. Teresa of Avila calls "experienced"). As St. Teresa says, "It is of great importance, then, that the director should be a prudent man—of sound understanding, I mean—and also an experienced one."[60] The rest of the characteristics are helpful, but not essential.

If you know and trust many Catholics who meet the above

criteria, don't be afraid to choose a small number of them to talk to about your vocation. Sometimes a well-formed person may simply not understand what you are saying, or they may not have had the experience you are having and are having a hard time understanding where you are. Sometimes they knew their vocation from a young age and therefore did not really ever go through the type of vocation discernment process you are experiencing. But as long as they are striving for holiness and they know and believe what the Church teaches, it does not hurt to speak to them. However, it is key that you speak to them over a period of time and not simply bounce from one to the next. The prophet Isaiah warns, "You are wearied with your many counsels; let them stand forth and save you" (Is 47:13).

Considering too many people as a director or spiritual guide can cause a kind of spiritual immodesty. We are not meant to reveal the inner movements of our heart to the whole world. Seeking guidance from too many people at one time would be like going to a large number of doctors at the same time. The different treatments they prescribe could conflict and cause greater problems. Just as it would be reasonable to see a few doctors about a certain unique condition, as long as they know that you are meeting with the other doctors, so also it would be reasonable to regularly talk to a few people about your vocation as long as they are aware that you are speaking to the others.

○ *Do's and Don'ts*

When discerning a vocation, you should have someone that you can talk to about this major life decision. That person should also be a stable mentor who can help you understand where God is calling you.

Do: Talk to Someone About Your Vocation

God chose to save human beings through human beings. Why? I'm not sure, but he's done it that way through all of history: think of Noah preserving his family and the animal kingdom, Moses saving the sons of Israel, Samson saving the Israelites, and most of all Jesus Christ, God become man, saving the human race. That salvation even continues today most clearly in his priests who administer the sacraments for the salvation of souls, and in a less clear way through all Christians who fulfill their call to "Go into all the world and preach the gospel" (Mk 16:15). If God desires humanity to be saved through humanity, then it only makes sense that he would want you to find your vocation—the way that he created you to become a saint—through a human being as well.

It does not matter what you call them: they can be your spiritual director, mentor, counselor, guide, whatever. The important thing is that they are striving for holiness and are well-formed Catholics. If you speak to them openly and honestly about the things that come up in prayer, the events in your life, your desires and thoughts, they will act like a mirror for you to see yourself more clearly and to see what God is doing within you more clearly.

Don't: Bounce Around Telling Everyone About What's Going on in Your Spiritual Life

God is calling all of you, your entire being, and it will require you to work with someone who knows you and your path of discernment well. If you only talk to someone once or twice about your vocation, the conversations won't yield all of their potential fruit. You need a person who knows all of you and what God has been doing within you over time. Talking to lots of different people about your vocation will force the conversations to be superficial. Getting fed up with a director because they didn't solve all of your problems in the first conversation and then moving on to someone else is a common temptation for people who really just want to get into their vocation. Stability is very important in the process of making a clear and determined decision about your vocation. It will help you to avoid the confusion and internal anguish that comes along with going down the path to enter into one vocation and then realizing at the last minute that it is not for you!

✪ Reflection/Discussion Questions

- Do you have some sort of spiritual director or guide that you can talk to about your vocation?

- If not, who are some people that may be good to talk to? Think of family members, family friends, your parish priest, a religious you know, or someone who works or volunteers at your parish.

- What topics do you most want to talk with a director or guide about? What do you not want to talk to them about, but probably should?

- Can you commit to regularly meeting with them over a long period of time?

CHAPTER 6

KNOW

○ Tom

Tom had graduated from college, was working a well-paid job, and was at that stage in his life when he was more than ready to be settled in a vocation. He spoke to me frequently about how he didn't feel at peace or settled in any particular location, because he didn't know what his vocation was. He would pray frequently about his vocation and fervently asked God to reveal it to him.

When I spoke with him more at length, it turned out that he wasn't actually doing anything to get to know any possible future vocation. He didn't have any friends outside of work and almost all of his friends at work were guys. He came home after work and just hung out at his house taking care of things, finishing up some work he had brought home, and watching Netflix. On the weekends he would play golf with a few of his buddies during the day and hang out with them and their families in the evening. When he went on vacation, he would go visit his family who lived in another state.

"So are there any girls that you know and are interested in?"

"Not really. But I know that if I'm called to marriage, God will send the right girl into my life."

"And if you're called to religious life, what orders do you think you might be called to?"

"I don't know. I don't know many orders, and I don't really feel called to the ones I do know."

"Do you think you are called to the priesthood?"

"I really love priests, and I know that's an amazing vocation, but I'm not sure if that's where God is calling *me*."

"Well Tom, how are you going to answer any of those questions if all you do is hang out with guys and married couples?"

Tom's attitude toward his vocation was very trusting of God and very pious, but it didn't really coincide with reality. Just as God can work through supernatural phenomena such as mystical voices (also known as "locutions") and visions, but it's better not to force him to that point, so also God can force your future spouse or religious order into your life through some miracle, but it's better not to get to that point.

The normal way that God reveals a vocation to someone is by that person feeling an attraction to a life or another person that they already know. That attraction eventually becomes solidified or fades away as they get to know the person or way of life more profoundly.

○ What Does "Knowing" Have to Do With Vocational Discernment?

"You will know the truth, and the truth will make you free" (Jn 8:32)

If a young lady was captured by her father and sent off to marry someone against her will, would you call that love? Of course not! Perhaps they would learn to love each other over time, but that act of marrying would certainly not be an act of love toward the husband. Why would it not be an act of love? Because it was not a free act. The young lady did not have freedom, and therefore she did not have love. True love can only be given freely.

Knowledge is so important in vocational discernment because love is so important in vocational discernment. Without knowledge of the truth, we are not free in the most real sense. Without freedom, we cannot love. Your vocation is specifically how God created you to love, and if you are not free to love as God created you to do so, you will not be able to properly discern how God created you to love.

To make things more concrete, suppose you are dying of hunger, and someone you do not know offers to give you either a hot dog or a steak. However, you have no concept whatsoever of what a steak is. You don't even know if a steak is food. What would you choose? A hot dog. Why? Because it is the only one of the two things offered that you know will fulfill your needs. Or even more so, what if you thought that steak was a poisonous chemical. What would you choose? A hot dog without thinking twice. Why? Because according to your understanding, a hot dog would be the only reasonable thing to accept in such a circumstance. And so, due to your lack of knowledge of what a steak really is, you end up eating an unfulfilling hot dog, instead of a big juicy steak.

The same can happen with a person's vocation. Due to a misconception concerning a certain vocation, a person may end up choosing the vocation that is not best for them but rather the only one they understand. They opt for the hot dog when they were really made to eat steak. For example, some men eliminate the idea of a priestly vocation because they have no idea of what a priest's life is like. Some women eliminate the idea of becoming a religious sister because they only have the concept of the grumpy nun who smacks children's knuckles. Similarly, some people eliminate the idea of marriage because their parent's marriage was so bad.

On the other hand, some people jump into a vocation without understanding the negative side of the vocation. Some men enter priesthood because they think that all you have to do all day is offer Mass and preach. Some people enter religious life because they think that then they won't have to deal with sinful people in their lives. And some people enter marriage because

69

they think that everything will be perfect—there will be no stress with work, their spouses will always agree with them, and their children will all be perfectly behaved. Such individuals are not freely discerning their vocation, because they do not really understand the vocation that they are rejecting or choosing. Every vocation has joys and crosses. We have to get to know people living each of the vocations in order to really understand that vocation well.

How do you get to know different vocations? By getting to know people who are living their vocation well. Therefore, everyone should do their best to get to know people who are living the married vocation well. Everyone should do their best to get to know people living religious life well. Everyone should do their best to get to know priests living their priesthood well.[61] By getting to know people who are good examples of the various vocations, we can begin to form a realistic understanding of each.

You Can't Love What You Don't Know

70

If a girl who never talked to other people complained to you that she had no friends, what would you tell her? Probably something along the lines of: "Well, start talking to people!" Relationships with people work in the exact same way as the story of the steak above: you can't love what you don't know. If you don't talk to someone, if you don't get to know them, then you won't ever love them, and they won't ever love you.

Pope St. John Paul II writes in *Love and Responsibility*, "A vocation always means some principal direction of love of a particular man or woman. . . . The process of self-giving remains most intimately united with spousal love. A person then gives himself to the other person."[62] Every vocation should in part be an experience of falling in love. You fall in love with a particular person and choose to dedicate yourself to him or her. You fall in love with a certain charism and community, and you choose to dedicate yourself to that particular charism and community. You fall in love with Jesus Christ in the sacraments and his priesthood, and you choose to dedicate yourself to Christ in the sacraments through the priesthood.

As we begin to know someone, we recognize them as either good or bad for us. If we see that they are good for us, then we are attracted, and if we see that they are bad for us, then we are repulsed. This principle can be applied to a vocation in general, such as married life or celibate life, yet it can also be applied to particular vocations such as marrying Jane, marrying Ben, entering the seminary for this diocese, or entering this religious order.

It is important to get to know different possibilities for our vocation but also to get to know good examples of people living those vocations. That means having healthy relationships with people of the opposite sex. It means getting to know the charism, community, and life of good religious orders. It means getting to know the life of a priest. This may require you to be very intentional and to put forth a real effort to get to know different people, different communities, and different priests. You might have to make trips to visit and work with different religious orders. You might have to go outside of your comfort zone to meet new people. You might have to volunteer at a parish to get to see what the priest's life is really like. All of these may sound difficult, but the knowledge that you gain in these experiences will make you freer in choosing a vocation and will make you a more experienced and understanding person.

71

Through these experiences of getting to know different concrete vocations to which God may be calling you, things will become much clearer. As you meet more people, there may be certain people that stand out as more attractive to one day be your spouse. As you get to know more religious orders, there will be a few of them that you really "click" with and some that you don't. As you work with priests, you will either be very attracted to the life of a priest or not at all. What you can expect is that there will be a kind of falling in love with a certain person, order, or life. Your heart will feel drawn to "some principal direction of love," as Pope St. John Paul II says, and that is a good sign that God may be calling you to that particular vocation.

Let's Be Real

Fairytales are wonderful stories, but real life does not often play out like one. Real life is wonderful, but it's also tough. Opening our eyes to reality will only help us to understand better what we are getting ourselves into with a vocation. If we well understand what we are getting ourselves into, we can better discern which vocation God created us for.

What can sometimes happen is that certain vocations become either idealized or villainized in our minds as we grow up. We may think that if we get married, our wife will never be emotional, the baby's diaper will never smell, the children will always be perfectly behaved, work will always go well, and our in-laws will always support us. Yeah right! That only happens in 1950s television shows. Real life will always have crosses. Every single vocation has its joys and its crosses. We're stuck with some sort of a cross no matter how we live our life and no matter what vocation we choose. Being Christian and doing God's will doesn't take away the crosses, it just teaches us how to carry them with us instead of dragging them behind us: "If any man would come after me, let him deny himself and take up his cross and follow me" (Mt 16:24). So discerning a vocation is not about avoiding crosses but rather choosing which kind of cross you want to embrace.

Every vocation also has great joys. Married life has the joys of passing through life with a particular person, deepening your love for them, living the joy of giving life to and raising children, growing old with your love, and eventually crossing the threshold of life next to them. Religious life has the joys of dedicating yourself completely to Love himself by the evangelical counsels, growing in sanctity with a particular group of people, having brothers and/or sisters to walk with you in a radical following of Christ, and loving people and Christ through them by the fulfillment of a particular charism. The diocesan priesthood has the joys of being conformed radically to Christ the Priest, dedicating your life in love to him and his Church, distributing the sacraments for the salvation of souls, working to build his Church in a particular location, and growing old knowing that you have sacrificed your life with Christ for the salvation of his people. Every vocation has great joys. Vocational discernment is much concerned with which joys a person is most drawn to.

We come to know the actual crosses and joys of a particular vocation by getting to know people living in that vocation now and by getting to know the concrete vocations that we could enter into; that is, marrying a particular person, entering a particular community, entering diocesan priesthood for a particular diocese. Having a lived experience of these vocations helps to dissipate the "fairytale image" or "nightmare image" of each of these vocations that we may have.

When getting to know people living the different vocations, don't be afraid to ask questions. What are the best parts of your vocation? What is the most difficult part? Why did you enter this vocation? What did you not expect to encounter in this vocation? What did you expect to encounter but have not encountered as of yet? The responses that people give you, if they are truly honest, can be very revealing. Also, be aware that not everyone communicates what is really going on inside them, either because they do not want to communicate everything or because they are not aware of everything. Observe them carefully and try to understand the answers to those questions. Ask yourself: "Could I live that vocation well?" "Could I embrace the crosses of that vocation with my whole heart?" "Are the joys of that vocation the most attractive to me?"

Also, when getting to know possible concrete vocations that you could enter into, such as people you could marry, orders you could join, or a diocese you could enter as a priest, ask yourself similar questions: "Do I want to embrace the crosses and joys of married life with this person?" "Is this person, with all of his or her personality traits and flaws, someone that I can love in an enduring way?" "Is this community and this charism the life that God created me to live?" "Is God calling me to be a priest in this particular diocese?" "Can I live this life with deep joy and love?" "Am I willing to embrace the foreseen and unforeseen crosses and joys of this life for the rest of my life?" The answers to these questions, when answered with prayer and reflection over time, will reveal God's will for our lives and strengthen us when it comes time to act in response to that call.

○ Do's and Don'ts

In order to discern between different things, we first have to know something about them. Get to know all of the different vocations. If you are a healthy person and really understand each of the vocations, they will all seem important and somewhat attractive. Don't just enter a vocation because you think it is important or good. Enter the vocation that is best for you.

74

Do: Learn About Each of the Vocations

"The mind of him who has understanding seeks knowledge" (Prv 15:14). If Jesus is "the way, and the truth, and the life" (Jn 14:6), then knowing the truth about vocations will show you both the way that God is calling you and the life he created you to live. Having an adequate and true understanding of the options sets up the possibility for a truly free and responsible choice. If you don't know, then you can't actually choose.

Everyone should get to know what married life is like when lived well, everyone should get to know what religious life is like when lived well, and all men should get to know what the priesthood is like when lived well before entering into any vocation. Everyone should also develop healthy relationships with other young men and women, with religious orders, and with priests. It is through those relationships that God typically reveals a person's vocation.

Don't: Choose a Vocation Just Because You Think It's Important

If you really understand each vocation, you will understand that they are all important and good. In fact, if you don't recognize that both the vocation to marriage and the vocation to celibacy are good and holy things, you probably shouldn't enter into any vocation, because you don't quite understand one of the two. God created marriage because "it is not good that the man should be alone" (Gn 2:18) and as the means for continuing human life through the millennia. Then Christ elevated marriage to be a participation in the mystery of Christ and the Church (see Eph 5:22–32). Marriage is a wonderful and holy thing!

Celibacy is an even higher good than marriage, because with celibacy we have an undivided heart for our Lord (see 1 Cor 7:32–34) and we live as the angels in heaven (see Lk 20:34–36; Mt 22:30; Mk 12:25). Paul suggests this in his letters (see 1 Cor 7:27–34), and in the book of Revelation, a special place is set aside for those who have dedicated themselves to our Lord through celibacy (Rev 14:3–4). Even higher than celibacy is the vocation to follow Christ radically in the evangelical councels through the vows of poverty, chastity, and obedience. The vocation to religious life is the highest of the vocations and is a beautiful life in which the person responds yes to Christ who says: "If you would be perfect, go, sell what you possess and give to the poor . . . and come, follow me" (Mt 19:21). All of these vocations are holy, all of these vocations are important, and all of these vocations bring the people who dedicate themselves to them to true sanctity. Discernment is not about figuring out which one is best or easiest but rather the one to which God is calling you, and the one for which God made you.

75

✪ Reflection/Discussion Questions

- Which of the vocations do you know the least about? How could you learn more about that vocation?

- Do you know good examples of married couples? Who are they?

- Do you know good examples of religious? Who are they?

- Do you know good examples of diocesan priests? Who are they?

- If God were to call you to married life, who are some people who you think could be good spouses? If he were to call you to religious life, to which orders do you think he might be calling you? If he were to call you to the diocesan priesthood, which diocese would you join?

CHAPTER 7

ACT

○ *Jude*

When I met Jude, he was already a grown man. He had worked a number of jobs, had traveled the world, and knew a little bit about everything. He was always at diocesan functions, and he had priest and bishop friends all over the country. He seemed like a good, responsible, and mature man, with only one odd thing about him: he wasn't settled in any particular vocation. He wasn't married, and he hadn't dedicated himself to celibacy. He was living as a life-long bachelor.[63]

We went out to eat after an ordination at the cathedral, and the topic of vocations inevitably came up. I told him my vocation story—how God had called me to the priesthood—and asked him where he was in his discernment. He started off saying he thinks he might be called to the priesthood, and then began to list off a number of reasons why. When I encouraged him to talk to a vocations director, he then started muddying the waters. Which diocese would he join? What if he's called to religious life? When I told him just to talk to someone and let them guide him through the discernment process, he then brought up the girl.

There was also a girl that he was interested in. But she lived in Chicago, his hometown, and he was living in Texas. They had been friends for years, but he had never really asked her out on a date. She had a great family, and they got along wonderfully, but he wasn't sure if he could be romantic with her, and the distance made it hard for them to get to know each other. Also, he thought he might be called to the priesthood, so he didn't want to begin dating a girl, because the thought of priesthood would always be in the back of his mind.

We eventually got to a point in the conversation where it was exceedingly clear to me that he thought he couldn't enter the seminary because he might be called to marriage, and he thought he couldn't date a girl because he thought he might be called to the priesthood, yet he wasn't willing to do anything to clarify either of the two options. When I playfully pointed the fact out, he responded, "Yeah, I know. . ." and then changed the topic.

I've kept up with Jude over the years, and he is still not in a particular vocation. He has changed jobs two more times since I first met him and is still "kind of" discerning the priesthood.

Jude is a man of prayer. He is striving for holiness. He has talked to people about his vocation. He knows the different vocations. But he is not willing to take the concrete actions to clarify his vocation. He is always afraid of taking the wrong step and so has ended up taking no steps at all and therefore has still not responded to God's will in his life.

What Does Action Have to Do With Vocational Discernment?

God Is a God of Action

God is anything and everything but indecisive. The Old Testament is filled with the actions of God. Think of God creating the universe, purifying the Earth through the flood, guiding Abraham, Isaac, and Jacob, calling Israel out of Egypt through Moses and Aaron, clearing the promised land, leading his people by the judges, anointing kings, rewarding faithfulness through victory and plenty, punishing sin through defeat and famine, rebuilding

Judea after the exiles, and preparing the way for a Messiah. The Old Testament writers frequently praise God for his works: "Sing praises to the LORD, for he has done gloriously" (Is 12:5); "Men shall proclaim the might of your awesome acts, and I will declare your greatness" (Ps 145:6); and "There is none like you, O LORD; you are great, and your name is great in might" (Jer 10:6). The pagan Greek philosophers said that God is pure act; there is no passivity in him. And the New Testament continues with the many acts of God. Think of Jesus teaching, moving from town to town, healing, suffering, dying, raising, and ascending into heaven. He then sent his disciples to act on his behalf: "As the Father has sent me, even so I send you" (Jn 20:21); "Go into all the world and preach the gospel" (Mk 16:15); and "Go therefore and make disciples of all nations, baptizing them in the name of the Father and of the Son and of the Holy Spirit, teaching them to observe all that I have commanded you" (Mt 28:19–20). God acts, and he expects us to do the same thing.

The Scriptures are continually calling us to action:

> But be doers of the word, and not hearers only, deceiving yourselves. (Jas 1:22)

> If you know these things, blessed are you if you do them. (Jn 13:17)

> The people who know their God shall stand firm and take action. (Dn 11:32)

> Not every one who says to me, "Lord, Lord," shall enter the kingdom of heaven, but he who does the will of my Father who is in heaven. (Mt 7:21)

> Every one then who hears these words of mine and does them will be like a wise man who built his house upon the rock. (Mt 7:24)

Think of the parable of the sheep and goats. The sheep are

welcomed into the kingdom of Christ's Father, and the goats are sent to the eternal fire. Why were the sheep welcomed into the kingdom of Christ's Father? Because they acted: "Come, O blessed of my Father, inherit the kingdom prepared for you from the foundation of the world; for I was hungry and you gave me food, I was thirsty and you gave me drink, I was a stranger and you welcomed me, I was naked and you clothed me, I was sick and you visited me, I was in prison and you came to me" (Mt 25:34–36). He doesn't say, "For you sat and discerned for your entire life whether you should give me food or not." He says, "You gave me food." You made a decision, and you carried out the action. Jesus makes it very clear that action is a necessary part of salvation. Our vocation is the path through which God wills that we be saved. So, if action is necessary for salvation, then it is also necessary in discerning and fulfilling our vocation.

The actions necessary for good vocational discernment can be broken into two stages. The first stage is when you are not in a situation in which you could enter a vocation. This could be because you are not at the adequate age or because you have not gotten to know enough about the different vocations to make a free and responsible choice.

During this stage, the actions required include getting to know different vocations through having healthy relationships with people of the opposite sex, getting to know different religious orders, and getting to know diocesan priests. These are all very low investment actions to take. If you live a normal life and socialize on occasion, you will probably develop relationships with people of the opposite sex. You can get to know different religious orders by volunteering at a nearby apostolate run by a religious order or making a weekend retreat at a nearby convent or monastery. If there are no religious orders near you, you could spend a weekend visiting and working with an active religious order. Orders are always happy to have the extra help! For the diocesan priesthood, you can simply volunteer at your parish, invite your local priest to dinner, or be involved in the other activities of the parish. The second stage of actions corresponds to the dedicated period of time spoken of in chapter 4 and will be discussed in the next section.

Be Not Afraid!

In the words of the Catholic thinker Peter Kreeft, "Great saints have often been made out of great sinners, but not one was ever made out of a wimp." The world is filled up with enough timid and mediocre people. What God wants is people who are willing to risk it all to do his will. If we think about it, we never truly risk anything if we are giving to God. God is never outdone in generosity. He always gives back to us much more than we give him. Whenever we take a risk to do his will, we receive in return "good measure, pressed down, shaken together, [and] running over" (Lk 6:38). Therefore, the fear of loss associated with giving our lives to our Lord in response to his call is unfounded. When it comes to our vocations, we should turn to the frequent exhortation of the Scriptures, often repeated by Pope St. John Paul II, "Be not afraid!"

In the second stage of action as we begin to seriously discern a particular vocation, doubt and fear can enter into our hearts. Pope St. John Paul II comments on the call of Moses as a depiction of how the process of discernment often progresses:

> We can learn how the Lord acts in every vocation (see Ex 3:1–12). First, he provokes a new awareness of his presence—the burning bush. When we begin to show an interest he calls us by name. When our answer becomes more specific and like Moses we say: "Here I am" (see v. 4), then he reveals more clearly both himself and his compassionate love for his people in need. Gradually he leads us to discover the practical way in which we should serve him: "I will send you." And usually it is then that fears and doubts come to disturb

81

us and make it more difficult to decide. It is then that we need to hear the Lord's assurance: "I am with you. Be not afraid!"[64]

In part, this fear may be a holy fear before the awesomeness of the vocation that God has laid before us, but we cannot allow even a holy fear to keep us from following God's will. Think of the Apostles at the Transfiguration. Matthew 17:6 says, "The disciples . . . fell on their faces, and were filled with awe." The Apostles were awestruck by what God had revealed to them, and they fell down in worship. However, in Matthew 17:7, the verse immediately following, Jesus tells them, "Rise, and have no fear." We should be struck by a holy fear before the awesome works of God, but it cannot paralyze us and keep us from acting according to God's will.

Therefore, when at a stage of life in which you are capable of entering into a particular vocation, and you have narrowed down where you think God may be calling you through the practices listed in this book, set aside a dedicated time to discern a particular vocation (review chapter 4 for more details). During this time, you should not only pray but also take concrete actions.

If you are discerning married life, the concrete action that has to happen is dating the person, or, as some people say, "courting" them. During this period, you should intentionally get to know the other well. Have intentional conversations about things that are important to you and are important for married life.

If you are discerning joining a religious order, you should get in contact with the order's vocations director or superior, make visits to the order, read more about the order's founder and charism, and spend an increased amount of time with our Lord in prayer discerning whether he is calling you to the "undivided heart" (see 1 Cor 7:34) of a celibate vocation.

For joining the diocesan seminary, the process is similar. You should get in contact with the diocese's vocations director, make visits to the seminary, read books on priestly discernment, and

82

spend an increased amount of time with our Lord in the Blessed Sacrament.

Lastly, during this dedicated period of time, you should cut off any relationships that you have that could inhibit the proper discernment of the particular vocation. For example, if you are dating a girl but really discerning entering seminary, you should break up with her. Seeing her on the weekends and receiving a flood of texts from her throughout the day will only confuse the discernment process. If you're called to marry her, then you'll recognize that you're not called to the priesthood. You can put that idea behind you and then start dating her again. If you are seriously discerning marrying a certain man, then don't make discernment visits to religious houses, and don't get on the phone frequently with the vocations director to talk about entering religious life. Those visits and talks will complicate and slow the discernment process. By following these guidelines, over time your desire for the particular vocation will likely increase or decrease. Your motives for choosing or rejecting that particular vocation will become purer, and you will likely come to a reasonable certainty whether God is calling you to that vocation or not.

83

When It's Time to Act, Act

By the end of the time you have dedicated to discernment, things are usually much more clear. Either you feel called to enter that vocation or you don't. If you do feel called to enter that vocation, then take the next step. If it is marriage, get engaged. If it is religious life, ask to enter as a postulant. If it is priesthood, ask to be accepted to the seminary. Don't waste time. The book of Proverbs says, "Do not say to your neighbor, 'Go, and come again, tomorrow I will give it'—when you have it with you" (Prv 3:28). If that is true of your neighbor, how much more true is it for God! If you are able to respond to his call now, and it seems that he is calling you now, then why would you wait until tomorrow?

If at the end of the period you do not feel called to that

vocation, then either God is telling you "I'm not calling you here" or "I'm not calling you here right now." In that case, you can turn to one of the other particular vocations that you thought was a possibility and set aside dedicated time to discern that vocation. You may feel pressure from the world to "hurry up and make a decision" or to "just get on with life." That pressure may wear on you. Do not make a rash decision just because you are tired of waiting: "Let us not grow weary in well-doing, for in due season we shall reap, if we do not lose heart" (Gal 6:9). Time spent discerning well is always time well spent.

So how do you know if you have enough certainty to take the next step in your vocation? First off, recognize what you are agreeing to. Asking to enter postulancy does not mean that you are making a lifelong commitment to become a religious. Formation to become a religious is typically a five-or-more year process. You have five plus years to test it out and see if God is in fact calling you to religious life. Asking to enter the seminary does not mean that you are definitely going to be a priest. Most seminary formation is six to nine years. Entering seminary is just taking the next step to discern whether God is calling you to be a priest. Becoming engaged is the highest commitment level of the three options. Typically, engagement is about a year, and backing out within a few months before marriage can get expensive (although it's well worth the cost if you realize you aren't called to marry that person!). The important point to remember is that this step is not the definitive step of choosing your vocation. Therefore, you don't need to be 100 percent certain that God is calling you to this vocation. You have time to figure that out. What you do need is enough certainty over time that God seems to be calling you in this direction.

So what constitutes enough certainty to take that next step? Don't expect a voice from God. St. Francis de Sales says it clearly: "We must not wait for the Divine Majesty to speak to us in some sensible way or that he send from heaven some Angel to point out his will for us."[65] What then is the sign that we should take the next step? Once again, St. Francis de Sales clarifies:

> A true vocation is nothing other than the firm and constant will possessed by the person called, to want to serve God in the manner and in the place where the Divine Majesty calls her. This is the best mark one could have to know when a vocation is true. . . . When I say "a firm and constant will to serve God," I do not mean that from the very beginning she would do everything that is necessary in her vocation with such a firmness and constancy of will that she is free of all repugnance, difficulty or distaste in what depends upon her. . . . Every human person is subject to such passions, changes, and ups and downs. . . . We must not judge the firmness and constancy of the will for a good that was earlier embraced, on the basis of such emotions and feelings. But we must consider whether among the variety of different feelings the will remains firm to the point of not leaving behind the good that it has embraced.[66]

Therefore, if through the discernment period for a particular vocation, your will to serve God through that particular vocation has continued or been strengthened, then that is a sure sign that God is calling you to take the next step. Of course, there are days when you will wake up and think, "That sounds like a lot of work. I don't really want to do that . . . ," or, "Do I really want to lock myself in to that life?" Those are the normal vicissitudes of human fickleness that take over all of us at times. The "firm and constant will" that St. Francis is talking about is the desire that remains when we are closest to our Lord in prayer and in the Sacraments and when we are well rested and healthy. It is the kind of "firm and constant will" that carries us to action despite how we feel on a given day or at a given time. When taking the next step to begin the path toward a particular vocation, do not be overly afraid of these small difficult moments. They happen to everyone, even though most people are too afraid to admit it. The time in formation or engagement will be sufficient time for you to understand those moments better, clarify any doubts, and continue to test that "firm and constant will."

◌ Do's and Don'ts

When it comes to action in vocational discernment, the key is to take the steps necessary to understand God's will. If God is not revealing his will to you through these steps, then simply be happy to wait until he does.

Do: Try Things Out (The Right Way!)

"Do not believe every spirit, but test the spirits to see whether they are of God" (1 Jn 4:1). How do you "test the spirits"? In vocational discernment, you do it by taking the next step to live the life. (This isn't the "bringing your relationship to the next level" that is sometimes spoken of in the world. God will never call you to commit sin in the discernment process). If you approach the new stage with prayer, a desire to fulfill God's will, and openness to your spiritual director, the "spirit" will manifest itself fairly clearly as the Holy Spirit or not. If you are not in a situation in which you could take concrete steps to enter into a vocation in the near future, then simply get to know the different vocations. If you are in a situation in which you could take concrete steps to enter into a vocation in the near future and you have narrowed down where you think God is calling you to a few options, then set aside a dedicated period of time to discern one of those vocations, always giving the benefit of the doubt to the higher vocations (i.e., first to religious life, then to the other celibate vocations, then to marriage). If in that dedicated time, your will to serve God through that vocation is constant or strengthened, then take the next step to discern: ask to enter postulancy in a religious order, apply to enter seminary, or get engaged. Remember, this next step is not the final step. It is still a time of "testing the spirits," so even if you are not 100 percent certain that God is calling you to that vocation, "Be not afraid!" Trust in God, continue discerning, and take the step necessary to keep moving forward in your discernment.

Don't: Think That Because God Isn't Telling You to Make Drastic Changes, He Isn't Responding to You

God's "thoughts are not your thoughts, neither are your ways [his] ways" (Is 55:8). Sometimes, we do everything right, and he just doesn't tell us anything. We got to know lots of different vocations, we narrowed it down to a few, we spent dedicated time discerning each of them, and each time it just didn't seem right. It can make us want to shout at the top of our lungs, "God, what's the deal!?"

The deal is: you're right where God wants you. How do you know? Because if he wanted you somewhere else, he would tell you. He is not telling you to go somewhere else. Therefore, he just wants you to stay put. This silence in response to our discernment is not a lack of an answer; it is God telling us not to go anywhere. As was made clear in chapter 4, timing is everything. God works on his own time. He understands all of the unforeseen circumstances, possibilities, and events in our lives and the lives of people around us. Sometimes he may have a vocation prepared for us, but for now he just wants us to stay put. This time is not wasted time, and it is not a time in which God has abandoned us. It is a time in which he is calling us to continue serving him in the situation in which we currently find ourselves.

✪ Reflection/Discussion Questions

- What stage of the discernment process are you in?

- What actions is God calling you to carry out to better discern your vocation?

- What is the next step in your discernment process?

- Is it time to move on to the next step of your vocation?

- What are the concrete steps that you need to take to move to that next step?

- What are the fears that you have to overcome in order to move to that next step?

CONCLUSION

Discernment is not a process like finding the solution to some mathematical formula. Just because you follow all of the steps and do everything right, it doesn't mean that you will immediately know where God is calling you and be able to follow that call immediately. However, there are several "best practices" and "pitfalls" that are pretty universal and which can either help to speed the discernment process along or hold it up, respectively. Therefore, to summarize what has already been said, here are the Dos and Don'ts in each of the areas of discernment:

○ You

Do: Be yourself when you are discerning. God is calling *you* to your vocation!

Don't: Choose a vocation to make someone else happy. You will be the one living your vocation for the rest of your life.

○ Holiness

Do: Strive for holiness now. God is calling you to be a saint now. Learning to respond well to God's fundamental call to holiness will help you to discern your particular call to a vocation.

Don't: Think that just because you are struggling with a given sin that you aren't called to a given vocation. Grace is real. Conversion is real. We need holy people in every vocation, so struggle with a particular sin doesn't mean a particular vocation is not possible but rather indicates the need for continued conversion and effort against the devil and his wiles, principally through prayer and regular reception of the sacraments.

○ *Prayer*

Do: Develop a prayer life for its own sake. Having a real relationship with God is necessary to live any vocation well. It's worth it to start working on it now!

Don't: Pray only about your vocation. God doesn't like telemarketing either.

○ *Time*

Do: Set aside a period of time to discern a particular vocation. Use that time to find the answer to the question: "God, are you calling me to enter *this* particular vocation *now?*"

Don't: Think that God has to answer your prayers during that period of time. God works on his own time. We can't force him to do what we want when we want it.

○ *Talk*

Do: Talk to someone about your vocation. They don't have to be called a "spiritual director," but it should be someone well-formed you can trust. It may also be a good idea to regularly speak to a few different people.

Don't: Bounce around telling everyone about what's going on in your spiritual life, hoping to find someone that will tell you exactly what God's will is. God is calling *you* (every aspect of you), and it will require someone who knows you well to be able to give you good advice.

◔ *Know*

Do: Learn about each of the vocations. The only way to get a clear understanding of what the life is actually like is to know the individual vocations. Have healthy relationships with men, women, priests, and religious.

Don't: Choose a vocation just because you think it's important, good, and beautiful. If you really understand each vocation, you will understand that they are all important, good, and beautiful, and we need good people in all of them.

◔ *Act*

Do: Try things out (the right way!). We can't test out our vocation just by imagining what it will be like. We need to live the testing period by setting aside a dedicated time to discern a particular vocation and taking the actions necessary to clarify any questions, doubts, or fears.

Don't: Think that because God isn't telling you to make drastic changes, that he isn't responding to you. Perhaps you're right where he wants you, and through the natural course of things, you will end up in the vocation he wants for you.

NOTES

1   Pope St. John Paul II, *Speech to representatives of the Parish Council and youth groups of the parish of Santa Maria in Aquiro* (Rome, February 8, 1987).

2   See St. Thomas Aquinas, *Summa Theologiae* I, q. 1, a. 8.

3   See Pope St. John Paul II, *Christifideles Laici*, no. 16.

4   Second Vatican Council, *Lumen Gentium*, no. 39

5   Oftentimes, Catholics will state things such as "I am called to marriage" or "I am called to celibacy." The mindset that God calls us to generalities such as marriage or celibacy whereas the particular person or community with whom or in which we live is secondary is very dangerous. God calls us to marry a particular person or to enter a particular community. I have directed many young people who temporarily refused to accept their vocation because they were convinced that they were called to marriage or celibacy. It was only once they accepted the idea that if God was calling them to a married vocation, it was with a particular person, or if God was calling them to a celibate vocation, it was with a particular community, that they were able to truly discern and enter into their vocation (sometimes even in the other category of vocations!).

6   Karol Wojtyla, *Love and Responsibility* (San Francisco: Ignatius Press, 1993), p. 256; see also Pope John Paul II, *General Audience of August 18, 1982.*

7   In St. Thomas, diocesan priests are not actually in the "state of perfection" (because they do not "sell everything they have and come follow [Christ]"). Only religious (because they take all three vows) and bishops (because they participate perfectly in Christ as priest, prophet, and king) are in the state of perfection. So when we're talking about an objective hierarchy of vocations, religious are actually higher than diocesan priests.

8   See St. Ambrose, *De officiis ministrorum*, 3, 12 (PL 16, 168); St. Jerome, *Ep. 130* (PL 22, 1118); and St. Augustine, *Sermo 148* (PL 38, 799), *Enarrationes in Psalmos 76* (PL 36, 970).

9   See St. Ignatius of Loyola, *Directoria Ignatiana Autographa*, no. 9, *Directoria*, 72; *Exercitia Spiritualia*, no. 15; St. Teresa of Avila, *Autobiography*, Ch. 3–4; St. Alphonsus de Liguori, *Counsels Concerning a Religious Vocation* in *The Great Means of Salvation and of Perfection* (Redemptorist Fathers, 1927), pp. 381–84.

10   See Pope St. John Paul II's Wednesday Audiences that make up what is now called the "Theology of the Body" (129 audiences between September 5, 1979 and November 28, 1984); see also *Familiaris Consortio.*

11   See St. Augustine, *De bono coniugali* (PL 40, 373); St. John Chrysostom, *De virginis* 10, 1 (PG 48, 540); Tertullian, *Ad uxorem* 2, 8, 6–7 (PL 1, 1412–13).

12   See St. Thomas Aquinas, *Summa contra gentiles*, IV, q. 58; St. Josemaria Escriva, *Christ Is Passing By*, nos. 22–24; *Conversations*, nos. 91–108; *Furrow*, nos. 797–811.

13   See *Gaudium et Spes*, nos. 47–52 ; *Lumen Gentium*, Chaps. II, IV.

14   St. Thomas Aquinas, *Summa Contra Gentiles*, q. 136.

15   St. Ignatius of Loyola, *Directoria Ignatiana Autographa*, no. 9.

16   Pope St. Paul VI, *Sacerdotalis caelibatus*, no. 19.

17   Pope St. Paul VI, *Sacerdotalis caelibatus*, no. 20.

18   Pope St. John Paul II, *Pastores Dabo Vobis*, no. 29.

19   St. Thomas Aquinas, *Commentary on the Sentences* I, d. 41, q. 1, a. 2, ad 3.

20   *Le Lettere di S. Caterina da Siena*, ed. N. Tommaseo, vol. IV (Firenze, 1860), p. 461.

21   Pope St. John Paul II, *Message to the seminarians of Spain* (Valencia, 8 November 1982).

22   W. Wright and J. Powers, *Francis de Sales and Jane de Chantal: Letters of Spiritual Direction*, trans. P. Thibert (New York, 1988), p. 111.

23   St. Alphonsus Liguori, *Praxis Confessarii*, ch. 7, n. 92. Emphasis added.

24   Second Vatican Council, *Lumen Gentium*, no. 11.3.

25   J. Ratzinger, *Compendium Catechism of the Catholic Church*, no. 428.

26   St. Josemaria Escrivá, *Furrow* (Scepter, 1987), no. 559. The paragraph goes on to say, "We have to teach, with the supernatural naturalness of Christian asceticism, that not even mystical phenomena mean abnormality. These phenomena have their own naturalness . . . just as other psychological or physiological things have theirs."

27   Ibid., no. 555.

28   See Aquinas, *Summa Theologiae* II-II, q. 23, a. 7.

29   Oftentimes celibacy and chastity are confused. Celibacy is the state of being not married. Therefore, everyone is born celibate and is only made not celibate when he or she enters into marriage. Chastity is the virtue of living our sexuality well according to our state in life. Therefore,

whether married or celibate, we are all called to live chastity, which consists in authentically loving everyone in soul and body according to our relationship with them. People most often fail in chastity when they begin to objectify or use their body or other people's bodies for their own gratification.

30   J.P. Camus, *The Spirit of St. Francis de Sales* (Longmans, 1887), p. 3.

31   See Aquinas, *Summa Theologiae* I-II, q. 58, a. 1.

32   "Sin is an offense against God: 'Against you, you alone, have I sinned, and done that which is evil in your sight.' Sin sets itself against God's love for us and turns our hearts away from it. Like the first sin, it is disobedience, a revolt against God through the will to become 'like gods,' knowing and determining good and evil. Sin is thus 'love of oneself even to contempt of God.' In this proud self-exaltation, sin is diametrically opposed to the obedience of Jesus, which achieves our salvation" (CCC 1850).

33   St. Ignatius of Loyola, one of the great saints who wrote much on discernment, describes his *Spiritual Exercises*, a thirty-day retreat created for vocational discernment, as "every way of preparing and disposing the soul to rid itself of all inordinate attachments, and, after it is rid of them, of seeking and finding the divine will as to the management of one's life for the salvation of one's soul." In more simple terms, this great saint wrote a thirty-day retreat based on the two steps of rooting sinful tendencies out of one's life and then discerning God's will.

34   Mother Teresa of Calcutta, *A Gift for God* (Harper & Row, 1975), p. 78.

35   *Compendium*, no. 299.

36   Pope St. John Paul II, *Meeting with the youth in Campo Ñu Guazú* (Asunción, May 18, 1988).

37   *Compendium*, no. 591.

38   John Henry Cardinal Newman, "Letter to the Duke of Norfolk,"V, in *Certain Difficulties felt by Anglicans in Catholic Teaching* II (Longmans Green, 1885), p. 248.

39   See Second Vatican Council, *Presbyterorum Ordinis*, no. 11: "The voice of the Lord who is calling, should not in the least be expected to come to the ears of a future priest in some extraordinary manner."; see also St. Francis de Sales, *Spiritual Conferences*, no. 313; Pope John Paul II, *Homily* (Benguela, June 9, 1992): "We must not wait for the Divine Majesty to speak to us in some sensible way or that he send from heaven some Angel to point out his will for us."

40   St. Evagrius Ponticus, *Pract. 49* (PG 40, 1245C).

41   St. Therese of Lisieux, *Manuscrits autobiographique*, C 25r.

42   St. Augustine, *Ep.* 130, 8, 17 (PL 33, 500).

43   St. Evagrius Ponticus, *De oration* 34 (PG 79, 1173).

44   Pope St. John Paul II, *Meeting with the youth in Campo Ñu Guazú* (Asunción, May 18, 1988).

45   For example, a parent, relative, teacher, or youth director.

46   See St. Ignatius of Loyola, *Directorium Definitive Approbatum*, no. 190, *Directoria*, 701.

47   See Ibid.

48   See St. Ignatius of Loyola, *Spiritual Exercises*, no. 175.

49   See A. Tanqueray, *The Spiritual Life*, nos. 1489–1513; see also St. Ignatius of Loyola, *Directorium Definitive Approbatum*, no. 203, *Directoria*, 707–8; *Annotationes P. Dávila*, nos. 134–35; *Directoria*, 519–20.

50   See the preface for distinction between subjectively and objectively better vocations.

97

51 See St. Ignatius of Loyola, *Directorium Definitive Approbatum*, no. 203, *Directoria*, 707–8; *Annotationes P. Dávila*, nos. 134–35, *Directoria*, 519–20.

52 M. Klages, *What to do with Helen Keller jokes: A feminist act* in *New Perspectives on Women and Comedy* (Routledge, 1992), p. 13.

53 St. Alphonsus Liguori uses the term *indifference* to describe what St. Francis de Sales calls "resignation": St. Alphonsus, "Sull'utilità degli esercizi spirituali fatti in solitudine," in *Opere Ascetiche*, vol. 3 (Giacinto Marietti, 1847), 616: "It is necessary for you to pray diligently to God to make you know his will as to what state he wants you in. But take notice that to have this light, you must pray to him with indifference. He who prays to God to enlighten him in regard to a state of life, but without indifference, and who, instead of conforming to the divine will, would sooner have God conform to his will, is like a pilot that pretends to wish his ship to advance, but in reality does not want it to: he throws his anchor into the sea, and then unfurls his sails. God neither gives light nor speaks his word to such persons. But if you entreat him with indifference and resolution to follow his will, God will make you know clearly what state is better for you."

54 See St. Francis de Sales, *Treatise on the Love of God*, Book 9, Ch. 4.

55 Pope St. John Paul II, *Homily at the Cathedral in Mexico City* (Mexico, January 26, 1979).

56 See St. Francis de Sales, *Spiritual Conferences*, no. 314.

57 See A. Tanqueray, *The Spiritual Life*, no. 534.

58 See St. John Cassian, *Conferences*, II, 5 (PL 49, 529).

59 See Ibid., II, 7 (PL 49, 534).

60 St. Teresa of Avila, *The Life of Teresa of Jesus*, trans. E. Peers, Ch. XIII.

61 Only men can become priests, but women should get to know priests who are living their vocation well for a variety of other reasons.

62 K. Wojtyla, *Love and Responsibility*, p. 256; see also Pope St. John Paul II, *General Audience of August 18, 1982*.

63 My understanding of a bachelor is specifically an uncommitted person. Single in the world is a valid celibate vocation (although, in my opinion, very dangerous when lived completely separate from a community), but only if they have made some sort of solemn commitment, usually before a bishop, to celibacy. Consecrated single life is a vocation that can bear great fruit in the apostolates of the Church. The Church could certainly use more faithful fully dedicated to evangelization and service. Imagine what good could be done by many consecrated single people who dedicated their lives to serving our Lord tirelessly in schools, universities, hospitals, and parishes!

64 Pope St. John Paul II, *Speech to the community of Santo Tomás University* (Manila, January 13, 1995).

65 St. Francis de Sales, *Spiritual Conferences*, no. 313; see also Pope John Paul II, *Homily* (Benguela, June 9, 1992); Second Vatican Council, *Presbyterorum Ordinis*, no. 11: "the voice of the Lord who is calling, should not in the least be expected to come to the ears of a future priest in some extraordinary manner."

66 St. Francis de Sales, *Spiritual Conferences*, no. 16. St. Francis is specifically speaking of a vocation to the religious life in this case, but the same can be applied to any vocation.

ABOUT THE AUTHOR

Fr. George Elliott, STL is a priest of the Diocese of Tyler, TX and Co-founder and Director of Catholic CAST Media. Discerning to enter the seminary while at the US Air Force Academy, he was sent to St. Charles Borromeo Seminary, where he served as a vocations envoy for one year, speaking about vocations at the high schools in the Archdiocese of Philadelphia. From there, he was sent to the North American College in Rome and studied Theology at the University of the Holy Cross and Patristics at the Augustinianum. While in Rome, Fr. George Elliott co-founded Catholic Bytes Podcast, which eventually became Catholic CAST Media. During his last years in Rome he served as the chaplain to the St. Lawrence International Youth Center and as chaplain to Christendom College's Rome Study Abroad program. He has worked in a parish as Parochial Vicar, Administrator, and Pastor. Now, he serves as a member of the diocesan vocations board, as the Chaplain to the Catholic Campus Ministry at Stephen F. Austin State University, and as Pastor of Sacred Heart Catholic Church.